T

D0847925

Writing Baseball
THE SOUTHERN ILLINOIS UNIVERSITY PRESS SERIES

BASEBALL'S NATURAL

BASEBALL'S
NATURAL
The Story of Eddie Waitkus

John Theodore
With a Foreword by Ira Berkow

Southern Illinois University Press
Carbondale and Edwardsville

Library of Congress Cataloging-in-Publication Data
Theodore, John, 1946–
    Baseball's natural : the story of Eddie Waitkus / John Theodore ; with a
foreword by Ira Berkow.
        p. cm. — (Writing baseball)
    1. Waitkus, Eddie, 1919–1972. 2. Baseball players—United States—
Biography. I. Title. II. Series.
GV865.W334 T54 2002
796.357'092—dc21
[B]
ISBN 0-8093-2450-4 (alk. paper)   20011057616

Printed on recycled paper. ♻

The paper used in this publication meets the minimum requirements of American National
Standard for Information Sciences—Permanence of Paper for Printed Library Materials,
ANSI Z39.48-1992. ∞

Writing Baseball Series Editor: Richard Peterson

To Maureen, Jackie, Meghan, and Mike,
for their loyalty and love.

To my mother,
for all those travels on the El to Wrigley Field, and

To my father,
for the Sunday doubleheaders at Comiskey Park.

Show me a hero and I will write you a tragedy.

—F. Scott Fitzgerald

Contents

Illustrations

Foreword

Ira Berkow

I had no idea she was there, lurking, as it were, in the crowd, perhaps even rubbing shoulders with me.

This was after Chicago Cubs games in Wrigley Field in 1948 and, particularly, Cubs–Philadelphia Phillies games in the spring of 1949. I was a boy of nine in 1949, she a girl of nineteen. We were both, it turned out, starry-eyed over the ballplayers—she over a particular player—as they came out of their clubhouses under the shaded stands, hair all showered and slicked back, looking like tanned gods and stuffed with thick shoulders into their light-colored sport jackets.

Most of them scribbled autographs for the swarming fans as they walked and then hurried on and disappeared inside their cars in the players' parking lot—or the team bus for the visiting players—leaving behind a trail of awe and aftershave lotion.

My friends and I went regularly from our neighborhood on the West Side of Chicago to the ball games at Wrigley Field and across town at Comiskey Park, home of the White Sox. All the players and coaches—anyone with a major league uniform—interested us, though of course we had our favorites. One of mine was Eddie Waitkus, a smooth-fielding first baseman who had been traded from the Cubs to the Phillies in the winter after the 1948 season—another one of those inexplicable Cubs trades that sent one of their best and most popular players away and doomed the team to perennial bottom-of-the-standings finishes. Waitkus was also her favorite but in a completely different way—in an obsessive, homicidal way, as it turned out.

Her name was Ruth Ann Steinhagen, and she lived with her parents and sister on the North Side, a short distance from Wrigley Field. While I was often in the crowd of fans that sought the autograph of Waitkus and others, Steinhagen, as John Theodore writes in the compelling narrative that follows, often stood apart, with bizarre thoughts running through her head.

I had a special attachment to Waitkus because I played first base, too, in our sandlot games. In my Lawndale neighborhood, it seemed that first base was less than a glamorous position. I was one of the younger kids in the games but tall for my age, and the older boys sought out pitcher, or short-stop, or center field. I'm not sure how I found my way to first base, but I did—I either gravitated to it or was shunted to it—and beseeched my parents to buy me a first baseman's glove, a three-fingered "claw" model. The glove was impractical in that you could only play one position with it. But I liked first base—you were, after all, in on most plays.

And I admired Waitkus, who had what I perceived even at that age as a cool and buttery style around the bag. He was left-handed, and I was a righty, but I still tried to emulate his unique, if somewhat comical, little midair jitterbug of stretching for a throw, catching a ball, and toeing the base all in one wondrous motion.

He was six feet tall, lean, with sharp Slavic features, and as I recall, from those long-ago days after games, warm, rather slanted eyes. And after games among the fans, he demonstrated a patience and bonhomie, though a slightly shy one, that many of the other players lacked.

Steinhagen was smitten with Waitkus, even built a shrine in her bedroom to him with photos of him. She learned Lithuanian because he was of Lithuanian descent. She wanted to marry him—though he had no idea she even existed—and knew that would never be. Her parents grew deeply concerned at the depth of the infatuation but thought it might just be a teen-ager's phase and would pass.

"As time went on, I just became nuttier and nuttier about the guy. I knew I would never get to know him in a normal way," she said in a report prepared by the chief of the Cook County behavioral clinic in response to an order from the felony court, which found her deranged. "And if I can't have him, nobody else can. And I decided I would kill him."

She purchased a secondhand rifle, checked into the pink, castlelike Edgewater Beach Hotel where the Phillies stayed while in Chicago, and sent a message to the front desk for Waitkus, signing it with a pseudonym. Waitkus, a bachelor, read the note, which asked him to come to her room, room 1297-A, and which said only that it was important. He found the note mysterious and decided to follow up. It was close to midnight, June 14, 1949.

Stories in the following day's newspapers that I and everyone else, I imagine, read with stunned disbelief described what had happened next. A banner headline in the *Chicago Tribune* read: "EDDIE WAITKUS SHOT; QUIZ GIRL."

The bullet that tore through the chest of Eddie Waitkus shortly after he walked into Ruth Ann Steinhagen's room ripped a hole through my idea—a nine-year-old boy's fantasy notion—that sports was not a part of the real world and that sports heroes were greater than mere mortals.

The rifle shot that exploded in that hotel room that night in Chicago, some ten miles from where I lived, remains with me, fifty-plus years later, and with the nation, as well. The incident is now not only a part of our national history—baseball with its long ties to our hearts and minds also indeed remains in many ways our national pastime—but it also provided a scene in our literature and in our print and celluloid mythology.

In one of the most dramatic moments in *The Natural*—a novel by Bernard Malamud, published in 1952, which years later was made into a Hollywood motion picture starring Robert Redford—an unsuspecting big league player named Roy Hobbs is shot in a hotel room by a woman, a stranger, wearing a black veil.

Fortunately, Waitkus survived. Not only that, but incredibly the following season, he was the star first baseman as the Phillies, known as "the Whiz Kids," went on to win the National League pennant. He batted a healthy .284 and played in every one of the team's 154 regular season games as well as in the four close World Series games that the Phillies lost to the Yankees.

How the shooting affected his life; how he was washed up as a baseball player after the 1955 season, at age thirty-five after an eleven-year career; how life began eventually to unravel for Waitkus personally, professionally, and physically is told in stark detail by Theodore. I knew little of this. But one day after having written a column on the passing of Waitkus and recalling the shooting, I received a letter from out of the blue from Edward Waitkus Jr., a lawyer living in Boulder, Colorado.

"In every dismal event," he wrote, "there is something positive which comes out of it. While recovering from the shooting my dad met my mother." This was in Clearwater Beach, Florida, where Waitkus was sent for rehabilitation and Carol Webel was vacationing with her parents, from Albany, New York. "Had it not been for this horrible event in his life, my sister and I would probably not be here. Life is very ironic. I think sometimes that all horror that comes to us has a reason. . . .

"It was a miraculous recovery from the shooting that Dad made, winning Comeback Player of the Year the following season and getting into the World Series. He said the Series was the high point of his career. . . .

"He had always told me he understood the four years of his career lost to serving in World War II. 'Everyone went,' he would say. He, however, never quite accepted being shot, that is, the time lost because of the shooting."

In a subsequent conversation, Ted Waitkus, as he is generally called, remembered as a boy feeling the deep indentation in his father's back that was made from the several surgical incisions required to save his life. His father told him that it was hard to believe that "a little bullet could make you feel as though six men had slammed you against the wall."

"My dad was an easy-going, trusting guy at the time and kind of flippant with women," said Ted Waitkus. "He walked into her hotel room and said something like, 'Well, babe, what's happening?'. . . . I guess she was a fanatic in the way the guy who shot John Lennon was. Then she went into the closet, took out the .22, and shot him. The first thing he said was, 'Why'd you do that?'"

The shooting, said Ted Waitkus, changed his father a great deal, "as you might imagine." He went from being "outgoing" to "almost paranoid about meeting new people."

On the morning of September 16, 1972—a little more than twenty-three years after the shooting—I opened the *New York Times* and happened to run across a modest-sized obituary notice on Edward Stephen Waitkus, former major league first baseman. He had died of cancer at age fifty-three.

I remember reading the Waitkus obituary and thinking how the shooting was the beginning of a heightened awareness for me of senseless violence and mindless, heart-breaking tragedy. Many more times I would experience the terrible gut feeling of helplessness, befuddlement, and rage over such events. It was there after the murders of John and Robert Kennedy and Martin Luther King, after the insane cult murders of Charles Manson and the preventable slaughters in Vietnam. It is there to this day with the genocides in eastern Europe and Africa, the mad suicide bombings in Israel, the seeming eternal conflicts in places like Northern Ireland, and the unspeakable attacks on the World Trade Center and the Pentagon.

But when I read the Waitkus obituary, it was only weeks after I had returned from the 1972 Olympics in Munich, where the eleven Israeli Olympians had been murdered by Arab terrorists.

I learned the phone number of Waitkus's younger sister, Stella Kasperwicz, and spoke with her. She told me Eddie had retained an interest in sports and had watched the Olympics. She said he had talked about the shooting of the Israelis.

"Eddie thought it was awful," Mrs. Kasperwicz recalled. "He said that none of us will ever be the same because of it."

I understood, I told her. I said I also felt that way about a similar incident that had occurred many years before, when I was a boy growing up in Chicago.

Acknowledgments

Baseball, many have said, will always endure because it is the perfect game. Perfection isn't what baseball is about. Baseball will always be with us because of imperfect heroes, characters who lure us into the past and subtly and passionately capture us forever. The greatest joy I had in researching and writing this book was being carried off to a different time, but newspapers, periodicals, and books offered only a glimpse at the past. The journey couldn't have been made without the many people who graciously shared their stories with me.

For some, it is very difficult to relive the past. I want to thank those people who reached back and talked with me about another time in their lives. I especially want to acknowledge the cooperation of the Eddie Waitkus family: Eddie's son, Ted Waitkus, his daughter, Ronni Barry, and their mother, Carol; and Eddie's sister, Stella Kasperwicz. Each had a unique perspective, and they all presented their stories with passion and dignity.

I can think of no greater sacrifice a person can make than fighting for his country on foreign soil. Angelo Dolce fought side-by-side with Eddie Waitkus in the Pacific theater during World War II. Angelo is still wrestling with nightmares from his war years. I know it was not easy for him to recall and recite his war experiences. But that's just what he did, and I'll be forever grateful to Angelo.

One morning my office telephone rang, and when I answered it, I heard an unmistakable voice bark, "Theodore, this is Ted Williams. You know, Eddie Waitkus was a hell of a man." It was vintage, straight-up Teddy Ballgame, war hero and baseball icon. He was gracious, caring, and inquisitive, asking me more questions than I asked him. As he talked, I found myself in another time, watching the Red Sox play the White Sox at Comiskey Park, my eyes glued on number 9 in the on-deck circle as he studied the pitcher. Williams and Waitkus were contemporaries, and it was Williams who gave Waitkus a job as hitting instructor at his youth baseball camp the last several years of Waitkus's life. I also want to acknowledge Fred Brown, a counselor with Waitkus at the Ted Williams Baseball Camp. Fred provided me with a valuable picture of Waitkus and his interaction with kids at a critical time in his life. Also, Steve Ferroli, a professional batting coach and Ted Williams's anointed hitting disciple, was able to reconstruct camp activity for me and present a younger perspective regarding Waitkus and how he hung onto baseball in the final summers of his life.

Lennie Merullo was able to reconstruct impeccably what it was like to play in the minor leagues in the waning years of the Great Depression. A teammate and friend of Waitkus in the minors and with the Chicago Cubs, Lennie was remarkable in his recollection and insight. I thank him for sharing his memories.

In addition, the following people allowed me to interview them for this book, and they, too, deserve my thanks: Dr. L. L. Braun, William Briska, Steve Buckley, Edward Barrett Colby, Dr. Howard Glassford, Buddy Hassett, Dick Johnson, Dr. F. P. Johnson, Ed Klama, Allen Lewis, Stan Lopata, Maje McDonnell, Russ Meyer, Bill Nicholson, Mary Meyer Oswalt, Belle Powers, Ralph Ricci, Jack Rockwell, Brooks Robinson, Father Simeon Saulenas, Eddie Sawyer, Andy Seminick, Frank Sharka, Mark Shapiro, Susan Shyshka, George Sullivan, Bill Vincent, Dr. Jerry Zadecki.

I wish to thank Chicago Cubs collector Doug Meyer for his generosity, especially with his photographs, and my sincere appreciation to my friend Steve Neal, political historian and *Chicago Sun-Times* columnist. Along with providing continuous support, Steve picked up most of the tabs during our research sessions at Harry Caray's.

My editor at Southern Illinois University Press, Richard "Pete" Peterson, deserves much recognition. Pete, editor of SIU Press's Writing Baseball series, had the patience and expertise to guide me through the long writing and editing process without ever losing sight of our shared vision. I sincerely thank him for that. Also, I want to express my appreciation to everyone at SIU Press; my experience with the professionals there was always enjoyable.

And finally, thanks to my wife, Maureen, and to our children, Jackie, Meghan, and Mike, for their unwavering support and for sharing the passion of baseball with me.

Introduction

One snowy New England afternoon a few years ago, the phone rang in the den at Lennie Merullo's Reading, Massachusetts, home. It was Hank Wyse, Merullo's teammate on the pennant-winning 1945 Chicago Cubs. "Out of the blue, Hank called," Merullo said. "I hadn't talked with him in twenty years." Wyse's health was failing, and he talked just above a whisper, but the two old ballplayers stayed on the phone for nearly an hour. They caught up on all the usual things—family, the way things, especially baseball, used to be, and, of course, they reminisced about their friends, players like Phil Cavarretta, Don Johnson, Andy Pafko. One of the first players they talked about was a Cubs first baseman named Eddie Waitkus.

"I was pitching one day, and Eddie booted an easy grounder, really bad, you know, kicked it all over the place," said Wyse. "He called time-out, walked over to the mound and slammed the ball in the pocket of my glove, and said, 'Let them try me again, Hank.'"

As the old pitcher talked, Merullo turned to a neatly framed photo on his wall. There they were, Waitkus and Merullo, somewhere in the minor leagues, clowning around for the camera in a 1933 Reo touring car. "You know, Hank, I can see Eddie now, sitting all by himself at the Commodore Bar in New York. A cigarette in one hand, a drink in the other, in a double-breasted suit with a boutonniere, maybe humming the latest show tune."

Eddie Waitkus played ball for most of his fifty-three years, including eleven seasons as a major leaguer. A self-taught, thinking man's player, Waitkus was a hero to some for surviving what life threw at him. Born and raised in working-class East Cambridge, Massachusetts, he was smart enough to attend Harvard, friends said, but he chose baseball instead. He survived World War II combat and played in the World Series, but he'll always be remembered for the tragedy that befell him on a warm summer night in Chicago in 1949.

"The first time I saw him, I was playing stickball with the neighborhood guys in front of Longfellow Grammar School in Cambridge," said Steve

Buckley. "It was 1970 or '71. I was maybe fourteen or fifteen, and there was this old man watching us. He was wearing green khaki pants and an old, beat-up and torn Phillies jacket. I had no idea who he was. One of my friends said, 'That's Eddie Waitkus, used to play for the Phillies.' I still didn't know who he was. But, before I knew it, he was standing behind me, giving me batting tips."

Each year since 1995, Steve Buckley, sports columnist for the *Boston Herald,* runs the Oldtime Baseball Game, a charity event held at St. Peter's Field in Cambridge. The players, mostly college kids, with a few high schoolers and a few old pros, wear throwback major league flannels. The game's official logo features a photo of a young Eddie Waitkus at first base.

Baseball keeps a shrine for its heroes—it's the Hall of Fame—but Waitkus isn't there. Baseball also embraces its heroic victims. One of them is Eddie Waitkus.

Major League Career Statistics for Eddie Waitkus

	YEAR	TEAM	GAMES	AT BATS	RUNS	HITS	2B	3B	HR	RBI	BB	SO	BA	FA
Regular Season	1941	Cubs	12	28	1	5	0	0	0	0	0	3	.179	.949
	1946	Cubs	113	441	50	134	24	5	4	55	23	14	.304	.996
	1947	Cubs	130	514	60	150	28	6	2	35	32	17	.292	.994
	1948	Cubs	139	562	87	166	27	10	7	44	43	19	.295	.992
	1949	Phillies	54	209	41	64	16	3	1	28	33	12	.306	.994
	1950	Phillies	154	641	102	182	32	5	2	44	55	29	.284	.993
	1951	Phillies	145	610	65	157	27	5	1	46	53	22	.257	.992
	1952	Phillies	146	499	51	144	29	4	2	49	64	23	.289	.991
	1953	Phillies	81	247	24	72	9	2	1	16	13	23	.291	.989
	1954	Orioles	95	311	35	88	17	4	2	33	28	25	.283	1.000
	1955	Orioles	38	85	2	22	1	1	0	9	11	10	.259	.974
	1955	Phillies	33	107	10	30	5	0	2	14	17	7	.280	.996
Career (11 Years)			1140	4254	528	1214	215	44	24	373	372	204	.285	.993
World Series	1950	Phillies	4	15	0	4	1	0	0	0	2	0	.267	1.000

BASEBALL'S NATURAL

1

Room 1297-A

Eddie Waitkus knelt in the on-deck circle near the first-base dugout and studied the Cubs' pitcher as he took his warm-ups. The intermittent drizzle and afternoon fog shrouded the infield, and the huge green scoreboard that sat atop the center-field bleachers was barely visible. His back to the field boxes, Waitkus cleaned the mud from his cleats and watched the pigeons dart in and out of the rafters in the darkened Wrigley Field grandstands, before eventually disappearing beyond the right-field foul pole.

The Phillies were on their way to another big inning, and Waitkus, a former Cub, was enjoying what would prove to be an easy victory over his old teammates. Waitkus walked slowly to the plate, unaware of the young woman in the white babushka in the first-base boxes. He reached out and slapped the first pitch over third base for a single.

Waitkus's swing was more smooth than powerful, with a spiral, upright turn to it, like a barber pole. An old-fashioned hitter, a thinking man's batter, Waitkus was a star at a time when young heroes like Stan Musial, Ted Williams, and Bob Feller gave postwar baseball elegance. It was a new era in 1949, and Waitkus, who had lost three major league seasons fighting in the Pacific, was part of it. In the middle of June, he was hitting .306 and enjoyed a huge lead—more than one thousand votes—in fan balloting for National League first basemen for the upcoming All Star game in Brooklyn.

When Waitkus rounded first base, the girl in the white babushka sprang to her feet, but she did not cheer along with the handful of Phillies fans sitting behind the visitors' dugout. Instead, she stared at Waitkus as he settled in at first base, and then she hurried out of the ballpark.

The taxicab carrying the two ballplayers turned north on Sheridan Road and pulled in front of the Edgewater Beach, an enchanting, medieval-looking pink hotel on the shores of Lake Michigan. The Edgewater Beach was the home to National League teams on road trips to Chicago. Club officials enjoyed the location, a five-minute bus ride to Wrigley Field; the players loved the Edgewater Beach nightlife.

Bill Nicholson and Eddie Waitkus were roommates and best of friends. Both players had been sent from the Cubs to the Phillies in the off-season of 1948, and at age thirty-four, Nicholson was a veteran of fourteen years in organized baseball. A large, affable man, "Swish" Nicholson's big, Ruthian swing from the left side of the plate made him the National League home run champion during the war years. Nicholson and Waitkus had just ended an evening of drinks and dinner at a North Side night spot with teammate Russ Meyer and his fiancée, Mary.

It was late, nearly half past eleven on a Tuesday night, but the Edgewater Beach was just hitting its stride. It was the most glamorous and seductive hotel in a city whose reputation, in part, was nourished after hours. The big-band sounds of Tommy Dorsey, Paul Whiteman, and Xavier Cugat filled the posh Marine Dining Room, where ladies and their escorts danced in formal dress. Outside, couples walked from the moonlit Beachwalk across a pier that took them over a sandy beach into the black lake.

Nicholson and Waitkus entered the sumptuous lobby of potted palm trees and butternut wood and headed for the Beachwalk. In this same lobby during the 1932 World Series, someone—an irate Cubs fan, the newspapers reported—spat at Mrs. Babe Ruth. The next day, her angry husband, according to baseball legend, pointed to Wrigley Field's center-field bleachers and hit the most famous home run of his career. A bellhop approached the two ballplayers and told Waitkus that a girl—he didn't get her name—had asked him to deliver a note to Waitkus. The note, the bellhop said, was in Waitkus's mailbox at the front desk.

Waitkus told Nicholson to go down to the Beachwalk and look for Meyer, that day's winning pitcher and also a former Cub; he'd catch up with them for a drink before bed check. At twenty-nine, Waitkus, lean and blond, the most debonair member of the Phillies, was considered a magician at first base because of his silky moves. He was just as smooth around women, who fell hard for his shy wit, urbane New England speech, and chiseled good looks.

2

Waitkus retrieved the handwritten note from the registration desk and began reading it as he made his way through the lobby:

June 14, 1949

Mr. Waitkus—

It's extremely important that I see you as soon as possible. We're not acquainted but I have something of importance to speak to you about. I think it would be to your advantage to let me explain it to you.

As I am leaving the hotel the day after tomorrow, I'd appreciate it greatly if you could see me as soon as possible.

May name is Ruth Anne Burns, and I'm in room 1297-A.

I realize that this is a little out of the ordinary, but as I said, it's rather important.

Please come soon. I won't take up much of your time.

No signature, just this strange request scratched out on hotel stationery. Waitkus returned to the front desk and got the attention of a reservation clerk. He introduced himself and asked who was registered in room 1297-A. He folded the note to the size of a matchbook and slipped it into a pocket of his camel's hair jacket as the girl looked through her card file.

He was told the room was registered under the name of Ruth Anne Burns, from Portland Street in Boston. The clerk also informed him that Burns had checked in the day before and planned to stay through the next day. Waitkus immediately felt uneasy. As a youngster, he had lived with his family on Portland Street in East Cambridge. Waitkus later told friends that he thought he was being drawn into something but could not figure out what.

Waitkus thought he'd better find Nicholson and Meyer and have that drink. He walked past the Marine Dining Room, where the next day the elderly, blue-haired ladies of Chicago's North Shore would take lunch. Waitkus found his two favorite teammates at a small table at the back of the Beachwalk. A light fog had started to roll in off the lake, hiding the long pier and the canopied swings that dotted the beach. Jack Cavan's band played a soft background as Louis Summers sang Cole Porter and white-coated waiters whisked away the sand flies from the dance floor.

Waitkus took the note from his jacket and tossed it on the table. For the next several minutes, the three ballplayers, according to Nicholson, dis-

3

cussed the bizarre note and decided Waitkus should give the girl a call before visiting her room. Most of the time, though, Nicholson said, they talked about Meyer's 9–2 victory that afternoon at Wrigley Field.

When they left the Beachwalk, Waitkus agreed to call Ruth Anne Burns in Room 1297-A. He later told Nicholson that when he called, he thought the girl had been sleeping.

It was nearly midnight when Waitkus set out to visit Ruth Anne Burns. He told Nicholson he needed to clear up this little mystery. "Maybe she's a family acquaintance from Boston and needs some help," he said.

When Waitkus left his friends, the fog had grown much heavier, covering most of the Beachwalk and crawling up the sides of the Edgewater Beach. When the elevator doors opened on the twelfth floor, Waitkus stepped onto the plush carpet and tried to figure out the most direct path to room 1297-A. He walked the length of two hallways before coming to a small corner vestibule that led to the room. He knocked twice before the door swung open.

The girl behind the door—young, tall, and attractive, her long, curling back hair held in perfect place by a flashy pair of studded combs—reconstructed her encounter with Eddie Waitkus for Chicago police:

"So I went to bed and after I had fallen asleep, all of a sudden I heard the telephone ring and I answered it and it was Waitkus." She said she asked him to give her a chance to get dressed, and when he arrived at the door a half hour later, she thanked him for coming.

"I know it's late at night for an athlete and all. Come on in."

She said Waitkus briskly walked past her into the tiny room and sat down in a small armchair near the room's only window, as she went into a closet.

"I have a surprise for you," she said from behind the door. She told police Waitkus was shocked when she came out waving a rifle in his face.

A machine gunner in four Pacific landings, Eddie Waitkus had faced death many times in World War II. And now a young girl in a white lace blouse owned his fate in a Chicago hotel room.

"What goes on here?" he asked. His back stiffened, and his face broke out in a twisted smile. "Is this some kind of joke? What have I done?"

The instincts that had kept him alive in war, the reactions that never failed him on the baseball field, vanished. The yellow flash tore through his chest and shoved him against the wall.

4

"I was so excited I could not control myself," the girl told police. "And then he slumped to the floor."

And the girl with the long black curls knelt by his side and held his hand on her lap.

2

Building a Dream

I've dreamt and dreamt about killing him, and there I was, holding him in my arms. Don't you see, all my dreams have come true?"

Ruth Ann Steinhagen sat at one end of a long table in an interrogation room at the Cook County jail. Cheerful and at ease, she enjoyed all the questions and was giddy with her new fame. The report to felony court from the psychiatrist who first interviewed Steinhagen described a young woman who appeared comfortable with her actions.

"One thing I'll say for Eddie, he always paid a lot of attention to me."

"When did he?" asked Dr. William Haines, the chief psychiatrist of the county behavior clinic. "When did he pay attention to you?"

"All the time. When we would walk down the street together he would talk to me. Not out loud, but in a mental sense, not physical. I didn't tell my mother because she would laugh at me. And if I told my father he would have sent me to a psychiatrist right away. But I did tell my girl friends.

"At no time did I actually feel him—I did mentally, but not in body. Mentally, I can recall him any time I want to. He has been in jail with me. I asked him, 'What are you going to do about me now? You wanted me to do this.' At the present time he evades me."

"Does he say anything to you, Ruth Ann?"

"He says, 'Don't you think it would be better if you went to some hospital?' I kept asking him over and over again how he felt about the whole thing, but he keeps evading me, so I got mad and didn't talk to him the rest of the night. That was last night, and that's the way it is now with Eddie and me."

On Sunday, April 27, 1947, Babe Ruth hunched over a microphone at Yankee Stadium's home plate and talked to the youth of America: "You know, this game of baseball comes up from the youth. . . . You've got to start from way down, at the bottom, when you're six or seven years old. You can't wait until you're fifteen or sixteen. You've got to let it grow with you, and if you're successful and you try hard enough, you're bound to come out on top."

The malignant tumor in the left side of his neck had continued to grow, despite efforts of a surgeon and radiation treatment. Ruth's voice was reduced to a croak, and his camel's hair coat draped a frail, ghostly figure that once was the most powerful and feared body in baseball.

The new commissioner of baseball, A. B. "Happy" Chandler, had designated the last Sunday in April Babe Ruth Day. Fifty-eight thousand people filled Yankee Stadium to see Ruth, and ballparks across America heard his raspy voice on public address systems. In August 1948, at the age of fifty-three, Babe Ruth would be dead.

Ruth Ann Steinhagen was part of a big crowd that went to Wrigley Field on that chilly Sunday. Up to then she had been a casual teenage baseball fan, going to some weekend games with Helen Farazis, her best friend since grade school. But this day would be different, according to Farazis's interview with Dr. Haines.

During the pregame warm-ups, when youngsters converged by the dugouts, trying to get autographs or at least the attention of players, life turned for Steinhagen. "Hello, funny face!" one of the girls near the first-base dugout yelled at Waitkus. He turned and looked at the girls, and from that time on, Farazis told Dr. Haines, Ruth Ann Steinhagen was interested in Eddie Waitkus.

As Babe Ruth's raspy voice cracked through Wrigley Field's loudspeakers, Ruth Ann Steinhagen began to build her dream. Two years later, she would tell Dr. Haines: "I had my first good look at him on April 27, 1947. I used to go to all the ball games to watch him. We used to wait for them to come out of the clubhouse after the game, and all the time I was watching I was building in my mind the idea of killing him."

The Steinhagen family lived in a small but immaculate apartment in a rundown neighborhood on Chicago's North Side, near DePaul University. In the history of her life that she penned from her jail cell—at the request of

Dr. Haines—Steinhagen wrote: "In my entire life, I don't think there's ever been one thing that turned out the way I wanted it to. Everything always seems to go against me." Yet as a child, Ruth was happy and well mannered. She enjoyed sharing her dolls and toys with her younger sister, but as she reached adolescence, she became more and more nervous. Crowds became enemies. She obsessed over the neatness of her hair and nails. She worried about the bugs that flew into her home at night. They couldn't be killed, she insisted; they were to be carried outdoors and released unharmed. But she also killed her family's pet canary. "I didn't mean to," she told her parents. "I just accidentally sat on him."

Boys were yet another source of confusion. She had a boyfriend that cared a great deal for her. He took her to ball games, even wanted to marry her, according to her mother. Ruth, though, was indifferent about him. She set dates with the boy but vanished when he arrived at her door. She felt unpopular in high school because sex wasn't important to her. That's why, she thought, the kids made fun of her.

Her sister, a year younger, was bored by baseball games, especially when Ruth made her stand in the hot sun after the games, waiting for the players to leave the park. But the practice of camping out by the clubhouse door soon became a ritual for Ruth and her friend, Helen. After each game, they found a spot on the sidewalk, just outside Wrigley Field's left-field wall. They waited under the trees on Waveland Avenue until, from below the bleachers, into the bright sunlight, the players appeared. The cluster of kids, mostly girls, chased after their favorite players. Some screamed their names, others laughed, and some politely asked for autographs. But what they all really wanted was to get close to their idols.

When interviewed by Dr. Haines, Helen Farazis revealed that she and Ruth often joked with each other as they waited—Ruth for Waitkus, and Helen for a young left-handed pitcher named Johnny Schmitz: "You trip him and I will drag him to a cab, take him to Crown Point and marry him," said Farazis. "Ballplayers were idols up in the sky, and the thought of sex just never entered our minds." But, Farazis added, when Eddie Waitkus emerged, Ruth Steinhagen always hid.

When the infatuation with Waitkus grew to obsession, the Steinhagen family were the first victims. For more than two years, Steinhagen followed his every move, and she learned all there was to know about him: He was from

Boston, so she ate baked beans and craved them daily; his jersey number was 36, so she canvassed the stores to buy records that were recorded in 1936; he was Lithuanian, so she bought books and taught herself the language and listened to Lithuanian radio programs.

She saw the movie *The Snake Pit* several times and became entranced with it. The film graphically portrays the life of a young, mentally ill girl who suffers horrifying experiences in a mental institution. Steinhagen told her family that one of the actors reminded her of Eddie Waitkus. And so did her boss. Steinhagen worked as a typist for a Loop insurance firm, but her nervous tension grew so unbearable that one November afternoon in 1948, she walked out of her office and gave no explanation. Steinhagen roamed the streets for hours. She later confessed to her mother that her supervisor looked like Waitkus, and that had made her upset.

She spent her nights starring at photos of Waitkus and kept a picture of the ballplayer under her pillow at night. "Why, do you know, she used to spread them out on the floor and look at them for hours," her mother told a friend. At dinner, she set an empty chair across from her—for Waitkus. One day, Steinhagen confessed to her mother, "I'm going to get a gun and shoot Eddie Waitkus, and then shoot myself."

Her parents convinced her to see a psychiatrist. She made two visits and stopped. But she started to make plans. When Waitkus was traded to the Phillies just prior to Christmas of 1948, Steinhagen cried for two days and then broke the news to her family—she was moving out—"to be closer to Eddie."

Up on the third floor, behind a frosted window, she kept a vigil in her new apartment. At night, a street lamp on Lincoln Avenue cast an eerie glow to the tiny room. Here she was alone with hundreds of Eddie Waitkus photographs and newspaper clippings, including game stories and box scores. She had fifty ticket stubs and scorecards from Cubs games at Wrigley Field and uniform emblems and pennants. On a small table next to her bed, in a gilt frame, there was a Sunday supplement photo of him. On one scorecard, she scribbled, "Eddie Waitkus is a schmoe." And in her diary, "Phils are losing. I bet it's none of our fault. . . I'll be glad when you're dead, you rascal you."

In early May, Steinhagen's plan began to take life, and Helen Farazis was there from the start. Ruth wanted to buy a revolver, Farazis told Dr. Haines, but when she learned she needed a permit, she decided to search the Chicago phone book for a nearby pawnshop. The psychiatrist's report to felony court outlined Steinhagen's preparations:

"At first patient wanted a revolver, but learned that she would have to have a permit. So she looked up pawnshops in the Red Book and finally went to a pawnshop where they bought a .22 rifle for $21. The man showed them how to take it apart and put it together again, and gave her two boxes of shells. She seemed pleased with it and handled it as though it were a new toy. She never said exactly what she wanted it for.

"On the Monday before the alleged offense the patient and informant got the gun and wrapped it up in heavy paper. She was not suspicious of it at the time, as it appeared to her as just a lark. They called a cab and went to the hotel, where patient had reserved a room. The following day they saw a baseball game, and both girls were happy. Nothing unusual occurred. They planned to leave the game together and she was to go the patient's room because she had stated that she did not like to pass all the wealthy women in the hotel lobby, because they looked at her.

"Then as the game progressed she appeared nervous and asked what if she should meet Eddie in the lobby. She knew she could not stand it, so she left the game early. The informant did not want to miss seeing Johnny walk out, so did not leave with her. She told the informant she was going to send a note to Eddie that night and ask him to meet her. The informant laughed, because she did not believe she would have nerve enough."

On June 14, everything was in place. Soon after Waitkus's single in the sixth inning, Steinhagen left Wrigley Field. If things were to go the way she planned, it was time to leave. Steinhagen gathered herself, took a final look at Waitkus, and hurried through the Wrigley Field concourse. She told police that during the short cab ride to the Edgewater Beach, she worked out the details one last time. She decided she would check the rifle again, put a bullet in it, and stand it up in the closet.

Once inside room 1297-A, Steinhagen called room service and ordered two whiskey sours and a daiquiri. She drank from each glass and fell asleep. As midnight neared, the phone on the little bedside table rang. The lives of Ruth Ann Steinhagen and Eddie Waitkus were about to intersect.

"For a minute I didn't think I shot him, because he just stood there, and then he crashed against the wall," Steinhagen matter-of-factly told Dr.

Haines. "I just looked at him. He kept saying, 'Baby, why did you do that?' And then I said, 'I don't believe I shot you.' He was still smiling.

"I asked him where he had been shot—I couldn't see a bullet hole or blood or anything. He said I shot him in the guts, and I was convinced he was shot. I don't know why. I thought, well now it's time to shoot myself, and I told him. Then I tried to find the bullets, but I couldn't find them, and I lost my nerve.

"I was frantic by that time and I called the operator to call the doctor. He kept moaning, 'Oh, baby, why did you do it? Why did you do it?' He was groaning and I didn't like that and I went in the hall.

"The doctor and the house detective came, and it was so silly. Nobody came out of their rooms. You would think they would all come out running. I got mad. I kept telling them I shot Eddie Waitkus, but they didn't know who Eddie Waitkus was. I thought they were just plain dumb if they didn't know whom Eddie Waitkus was.

"After that the police came, but I was burning because nobody was coming out of those other rooms. Nobody seemed to want me much. I could have walked right out of the place and nobody would have come after me."

3

A Sealed Fate

On June 15, 1949, Chicagoans awoke to a three-inch banner headline on the front page of the *Chicago Daily Tribune:* "EDDIE WAITKUS SHOT; QUIZ GIRL." The bulletin below tried to make sense of the event: "Miss Ruth Steinhagen, 19, of 1950 Lincoln av. admitted that she shot Eddie Waitkus, Police Capt. John T. Warren said. She earlier had given her name as Ruth Anne Burns and told a confused story, Warren said. Waitkus said he never had seen the girl before last night."

Waitkus's friends were shaken by the shooting. The Phillies' Russ Meyer and Bill Nicholson and Phil Cavarretta of the Cubs tried to organize a prayer vigil at the hospital, but doctors said no. "He's one of the sweetest guys I ever knew," Nicholson said. "I never got such a shock in my life. He's not the kind of man who goes around getting in trouble. I've been in baseball fifteen years and never roomed with a finer guy."

Waitkus was shot in the right side of the chest, just below the nipple. The bullet pierced the lung and lodged in muscle near the spine. He was bleeding in the right lung but conscious when the ambulance brought him to Illinois Masonic Hospital's emergency entrance. "I guess the gal wasn't a Phillies fan," he said to a nurse.

The path the bullet took as it spun through his body proved to be miraculously lucky for Waitkus. Any caliber other than a .22, doctors agreed, would have caused instant death. The small bullet slipped cleanly between two ribs. It missed the arteries, veins, and nerves that run on the underside of each rib. It ripped a hole in his right lung, collapsing it, but managed to travel relatively harmlessly again between the ribs in his back, hitting no major blood vessels. The bullet also missed the spine, finally stopping in thick back muscles.

Initial blood test told him there appeared to be no massive internal bleeding, but Dr. L. L. Braun, the Cubs' team physician who first treated Waitkus at the hospital, wasn't optimistic. "It's touch and go whether he'll live," he told reporters. But Braun also knew that a young athlete's body has an amazing power to keep its integrity when injured. He was confident Waitkus could lose a great deal of blood before the bottom would fall out.

At half past two in the morning, that was about to happen. In the middle of the night, with Waitkus's condition stabilized, an unmarked police car pulled up alongside Illinois Masonic's side entrance. Captain John Warren and Ruth Ann Steinhagen slipped past reporters and quietly took the stairwell to the second-floor nurses' station. Warren told a nurse he needed a positive identification. Waitkus heard their footsteps and turned his head toward the door. He saw the long shadow in the dimly lit hallway and his blood froze. Again, she came at him. Warren held Steinhagen's arm as she entered the dark room and stepped close to the bed.

"Why did you do it?" Waitkus could barely get the words out, but he managed to point directly at her.

"I'm not sure," she said softly and turned away.

In a matter of seconds, Waitkus went into shock and his body struggled to hold itself together. His blood pressure dropped to eighty over forty, his pulse raced to over 130, and he coughed up blood. The lower lobe in his right lung had collapsed and was filling with blood. Doctors gave Waitkus oxygen, and the foot of his bed was raised off the floor and placed on wood "shock blocks" to help move blood to his brain and heart. He also received five hundred cubic centimeters of blood through an IV. Throughout the night, nurses kept a close watch. They monitored his blood pressure and pulse every few minutes and checked his color.

By nine that morning, Waitkus's mental status had improved dramatically, and his blood pressure and pulse had stabilized. He was given a solution of saline, potassium, calcium, and vitamins; his medication was penicillin and codeine. "Nothing short of a miracle," was how his doctors described his incredible physical recovery. X-rays revealed that Waitkus was bleeding slowly into his chest from his right lung, but Dr. Braun determined that immediate surgery was not necessary. He decided to follow a "conservative management course."

Waitkus eventually underwent two painful operations at Illinois Masonic to drain the accumulation of blood from his right lung. In the procedure, known as thoracentesis, a five-inch needle was inserted in his chest to drain nearly six hundred cubic centimeters of blood. Doctors, though, were cautious about removing the bullet. The initial X-ray report revealed "a metallic foreign body, the size of a twenty two caliber bullet, at approximately level of the interspace between the ninth and tenth dorsal vertebrae, overshadowing the right margins of the segments, however, the exact depth of nearness to the spine is not clearly discernable."

Since there did not appear to be any serious infection, doctors decided to wait until Waitkus's lung was stronger before removing the bullet.

On June 17, three days after the shooting, the physician's orders in Waitkus's hospital chart read: "patient feels well, is alert and seems to be breathing easier." That afternoon, looking tired and pale, Waitkus faced reporters in his room. Although he still had a difficult time breathing, he tried to be glib. "I still haven't got over the whole surprise. It's just like a bad dream. I would like to know what got into that silly honey picking on a nice guy like me. She must be crazy charging around with a rifle." Referring to his World War II experience, he told reporters, "It was safer in New Guinea, wasn't it?"

The writers had only five minutes to question Waitkus. To a man, they wanted to know why he had decided to visit the girl.

"I called her room out of curiosity," he said. "The girl said she wanted to see me on something important. I thought it might be someone I knew, or a friend of a friend. When she opened the door, she took a look and said, 'Come on in for a minute.' She was very abrupt and businesslike. I asked what she wanted and walked through the little hall over to the window.

"When I turned around, there she was with this rifle. She had the coldest looking face I ever saw. No expression at all. She wasn't happy; she wasn't anything. She said, 'you're not going to bother me any more.' Before I could say anything, whammy!

"When I first saw the rifle, I thought it was somebody's idea of a practical joke, maybe some of the players might have put her up to a 'hey, Mabel!' gag. I guess I zigged when I should have zagged."

There is no evidence any reporter asked Waitkus specifically if he knew a girl by the name of Ruth Anne Burns from Boston. He told them right from the start, "It might be someone I knew," but there was never any follow-up by the press. And there is nothing on record to indicate the police ever asked Ruth Ann Steinhagen why she used that particular name. Because she knew so much about Waitkus's past, Steinhagen probably read about Waitkus's East Cambridge friend, Jack Burns, a former major league first baseman with the St. Louis Browns. On one of the pages of Waitkus's 1935 Cambridge High and Latin School yearbook is a black-and-white photo of the senior drama class. In the front row, the tallest of five girls—Ruth Burns—wears a beaded comb in her black, curling hair. At first glance, she bears a striking resemblance to a tall, slender, nineteen-year-old Ruth Ann Steinhagen. Because of her obsessive, detailed research on Waitkus, it is conceivable that Steinhagen had obtained a copy of the high school yearbook and found the look-alike photo of Burns. Ruth Burns was an acquaintance of Waitkus, a girl he knew in high school, nothing more. But for Steinhagen, the name Ruth Burns became the final piece to her deranged plan to lure Waitkus to her tiny room at the Edgewater Beach Hotel.

At the foot of Waitkus's hospital bed, postal bags from that morning's mail contained more than four hundred cards and letters from fans across the country. Across town, at Cook County jail, that "silly honey," Ruth Ann Steinhagen, told authorities, "I've never been so happy in my life."

Waitkus spent a full month in the hospital. At the beginning of July, he was sent to Billings Memorial Hospital on the campus of the University of Chicago. There, doctors performed a third operation to re-expand his partially collapsed lung. A persistent fever then made it necessary to remove the bullet. The stress was beginning to show as Waitkus began yet another adventure—an inward journey, against a fear he would never again play baseball.

Meanwhile, the *Chicago Daily Tribune* published "Waitkus' Assailant at Play," a bizarre photo spread of Steinhagen playing baseball at the county jail's recreation yard. "She seems to think this is some kind of a joke, but I don't," Waitkus said when he saw the newspaper. "She should be taken off the streets—the same as a mad dog."

Waitkus received more than three thousand cards, letters, and telegrams from well-wishers, some from people who said they had never seen a baseball game. When he arrived back in Philadelphia on July 17, five hundred fans braved an all-day rain to greet him at the airport. Soft-spoken but not shy, Waitkus never craved adulation, and he relied on a coy sense of humor in uneasy situations. "Can't let a girl get you down," he told the crowd. "What gets me, though, is that this was the only girl in the world who thought I was perfect, and now they say she's crazy."

4

A Swift Judgement Day

Behind bars at the county jail, Ruth Ann Steinhagen wrote her life story, on orders from Dr. William Haines, the court-appointed psychiatrist. She arranged a small workspace against her cell bars with books, an embroidered white tablecloth, and a photo of Waitkus in his hospital bed.

"The first year I was crazy about him," she explained. "I had my first good look at him in 1947. I used to go to all the ballgames just to watch him. We used to wait for them to come out of the clubhouse after the game, and all the time I was watching him, I was building in my mind the idea of killing him. As time went on, I just became nuttier and nuttier about the guy. I knew I would never get to know him in a normal way, so I kept thinking I will never get him, and if I can't have him, nobody else can. Then I decided I would kill him. I didn't know how or when, but I knew I would kill him.

"After a year went by and I was still crazy about him I decided to do something about it. Then I decided to kill him with a gun it would be the easiest way. I actually got the gun in May. I didn't think I would have the courage to get a gun, because I am afraid of one. I knew I couldn't get a small gun like I wanted because you have to go through the trouble of getting a permit, so I went to the pawnshop and got this second-hand rifle. My girlfriend was with me at the time. After that I looked up the schedule to see when the Phillies would be here. I knew they were staying at the hotel, so I put my reservation in for the time they would be there. I got the reservation and it was just a question of waiting. During that time I learned how to put it together and take it apart. Then I just waited until it was time to go."

Steinhagen seemed to relish the writing assignment and all the interviews with Dr. Haines. Shortly after the shooting, she told police at the Summerdale station that she originally had crushes on movie star Alan Ladd and Cubs infielder Peanuts Lowrey. Steinhagen gave police nine statements, each one different as to the reason she tried to kill Waitkus. "She changed her story every time she rolled her eyes," Sergeant Nick Reidy said.

When Steinhagen re-enacted the shooting for police, she showed them how she planned to kill herself with a paring knife after she shot Waitkus, but she lost her nerve. When police searched room 1297-A, they found a crumpled piece of paper in the wastebasket, which they believed was a suicide note Steinhagen wrote to her parents: "I hope you understand things. . . . I love you. . . . Things will turn out for the best."

"It's lucky for Mr. Waitkus she failed to commit suicide or he may have had a lot of trouble clearing himself of the scandal," said Reidy.

Steinhagen was given several psychological tests; her IQ was determined to be 99. "There is a noted lack of social intelligence," Dr. Haines reported to the court. "On the Rorschach test, a summary reveals that there are indications of a childlike emotional status, incapable of meeting personality conflicts. Her pseudo-solution has been to use reality selectively. It is felt that this investigation indicates an incipient schizophrenic psychosis."

Steinhagen's violent plan had festered inside her for more than two years. But her day of judgement—June 30, just two weeks from the night of the shooting—was swift in coming. The visitors' gallery in the felony courtroom of Judge Matthew Hartigan was filled to capacity for Steinhagen's hearing. Dressed in a blue suit and a blue-and-yellow tie, Eddie Waitkus was brought into the courtroom in a wheelchair. He calmly told the judge how he went to room 1297-A just before midnight in response to a note saying it was important that he see Ruth Anne Burns. Waitkus was under control as he relived the episode for the court, but he never spoke to Steinhagen, who sat with her two attorneys. Dressed in a chartreuse blouse, a black ballerina skirt with deep pockets, and green alligator high-heel shoes, she showed no emotion and chewed gum rhythmically during the entire hearing.

The girl's father, Walter G. Steinhagen, stood near his daughter during the hearing. At one point, he edged close to Waitkus and whispered, "Did you receive my note?" He was referring to an apology he had sent to Waitkus's hospital room. Waitkus turned and answered, "Yes." Afterward, he told the press, "I didn't want to talk to anyone, let alone any member of her family."

Once Waitkus testified, Steinhagen's attorneys—George Bieber and Michael Brodkin—waived cross-examination, but they asked the judge that Dr. Haines's report be made part of the record. Steinhagen's bond was set at $50,000, and she was held for the Cook County grand jury on a charge of assault with intent to murder. Waitkus was wheeled to the grand jury room, and almost immediately, the grand jury returned a true bill indictment.

"Ruth Steinhagen," indictment number 49-1303 read, "was armed with a certain rifle then and there charged with gunpowder and drivers leaden bullets, which rifle then and there was a dangerous and deadly weapon; and that said Ruth Steinhagen then and there unlawfully, feloniously, wilfully and maliciously made an assault with said rifle in and upon Eddie Waitkus, who then and there was in the peace of the People of said State of Illinois, with an intent on the part of said Ruth Steinhagen then and there unlawfully, feloniously, wilfully and with malice of aforethought to kill and murder said Eddie Waitkus; contrary to the Statute, and against the peace and dignity of the same People of the State of Illinois."

Steinhagen's attorneys, with her parents' consent, had prepared a petition to present to the court once she was indicted. It stated that Steinhagen was "unable to cooperate with her counsel in the defense of her cause" and did not "understand the nature of the charge against her." It asked for a sanity hearing.

Dr. Haines told the court at the sanity hearing that he had examined Steinhagen daily and found her insane. His diagnosis: "Schizophrenia in an immature individual. She is committable to an institution for the mentally ill. At no time does she show concern, nor appear to realize the seriousness of her behavior. She discusses suicide freely and has thought of many methods that she would try. She should be under constant surveillance." With that, the chief justice of the Criminal Court of Cook County, Judge James McDermott, directed the jury to find her insane. The indictment against her was stricken with leave to reinstate, meaning she could be brought to trial on the assault with intent to commit murder if she recovered her sanity. Ruth Ann Steinhagen, age nineteen, continued to chew her gum, and she displayed no emotion when McDermott committed her to the Kankakee State Hospital. The entire judicial process took three hours.

An exhausted Waitkus was driven back to Illinois Masonic shortly before noon. Needing help from nurses to change from his blue suit to his hospital robe, Waitkus collapsed on his bed and said, "Gee, that was terrible. Worse than a doubleheader in August."

The drive south to Kankakee took Steinhagen through rolling Illinois farmland. Red and green barns stood alongside white farmhouses with wide front porches, kids played on swing sets, and laundry waved in the warm breeze. It was a world away from Wrigley Field, Lincoln Avenue, and the Edgewater Beach Hotel. It was a calm summer's day, and Ruth Ann Steinhagen, in the back seat of a state-owned sedan, held a shopping bag of belongings on her lap and headed for her strange new realm.

5

East Cambridge and Beyond

The bizarre incident at the Edgewater Beach shocked baseball fans across the country and sealed the fate of Eddie Waitkus. Three years later, it even became part of baseball folklore. In 1952, Bernard Malamud fictionalized the shooting in his book *The Natural*. Malamud's young hero, Roy Hobbs, pursuer of the American baseball dream, is drawn into a woman's hotel room. "Roy," he's sweetly asked, "will you be the best there ever was in the game?" Then, inexplicably, he is shot.

In 1949, baseball was very much the American dream. An ailing Joe DiMaggio had become the first baseball player to earn a salary of $100,000 a season. He watched from the Yankee dugout on opening day as his club unveiled a stone monument to Babe Ruth in center field. The inscription: "A great ball player. A great man. A great American." It towered over plaques of past Yankee icons Lou Gehrig and Miller Huggins, Ruth's manager. Weeks later, the Yankees signed a seventeen-year-old high school star from Oklahoma—Mickey Mantle—for $1,000.

In 1949, baseball commissioner Happy Chandler sold the World Series radio and television rights to the Gillette Safety Razor Company for $1,000,000. Baseball was also inspiration that year for the silver screen and its biggest stars. At least four hit movies used baseball as a theme: *Take Me Out to the Ball Game,* a musical with Frank Sinatra, Gene Kelly, and Jules Munshin; *It Happens Every Spring,* a comedy with Ray Milland and Jean Peters; *The Stratton Story,* with Jimmy Stewart and June Allyson; and *The Kid from Cleveland,* featuring Lou Boudreau, Satchel Paige, and Indians owner Bill Veeck.

Waitkus was approaching the zenith of his career in 1949 when he was shot. Because of his strong, quick wrists, he was a line-drive doubles hitter. But it was his silky-smooth glove that drew most of the attention. "With Waitkus on first," said Philadelphia shortstop Granny Hamner, "you don't have to waste any time aiming the ball before you throw. You just let it fly. You know that if it's in the right general direction, Eddie will come up with it." Willie "Puddin' Head" Jones, the Phillies' third baseman, also appreciated Waitkus's skills at first. "I don't know how many times I apologized and thanked him," Jones said after the shooting. "Just as soon as a wild throw left my hand I knew he was in trouble. But somehow he got it. It was funny how those two thoughts would go through my mind—'oh-uh—there it goes against the grandstand' . . . and then . . . 'Oh, Eddie will get it.'"

Waitkus was also highly intelligent, with a good-natured wit. He read Latin, spoke four languages, and went to the opera. He also enjoyed night-clubbing and fine restaurants—Coconut Grove in Boston, Bookbinder's in Philadelphia, and the Chez Paree in Chicago. He quoted poetry and was sentimental over songs. His suits were tailor made, his coats cashmere. Being a handsome bachelor, Waitkus was often seen in the company of beautiful women. Waitkus not only handled himself well around the opposite sex, he also enjoyed a very good relationship with the press. When a good-looking ballplayer is caught visiting the hotel room of a nineteen-year-old girl at midnight, rumors spread. But Chicago writer Edward Burns of the *Tribune* knew Waitkus well when he was on the Cubs, and he was first to protect Waitkus's reputation: "Expressions of what Waitkus' loss might mean to the Phillies were withheld during the hours of anxiety and stunned wonderment that such a misfortune could befall a well-behaved lad like Eddie." In New York, the *Word-Telegram* wrote: "Brooklyn players are shocked by the Eddie Waitkus shooting. A happy-go-lucky sort, Waitkus is well liked around the league. He was one of the first opposing players to befriend Jackie Robinson." "Ever since the popular Waitkus came to the Phils," the Associated Press reported, "his defensive play and timely and consistent hitting have established him in the minds of the players, as well as officials of the club, as the best first baseman in the National League."

While reporters wrote about how well-liked Waitkus was among National League players and the press, the initial comments from the Phillies' rookie manager focused on what the loss of Waitkus meant to his team. The day after the shooting, Eddie Sawyer, a tough, shoot-from-the-hip man who never let sentiment get in the way of his job, leaned against the Wrigley Field batting cage before the game and told reporters, "What a break against us. We've got Dick Sisler to take Eddie's place, and he can hit the ball out of the park. But Waitkus has everything." And decades later, this perspective hadn't changed: "I guess the gal was interested in a few guys, even a movie star if I remember. But she had to shoot my first baseman."

Edward Stephen Waitkus was born on September 4, 1919, in Cambridge, Massachusetts, to Veronica and Stephen Waitkus, Lithuanian immigrants who met and fell in love on their passage to America. The family lived in a modest flat in East Cambridge, and Waitkus's boyhood world was within the blocks surrounding his home. He was an altar boy at St. Patrick's Roman Catholic Church, attended Kelley Grammar School, and played ball at Cambridge Field. "Eddie was always playing baseball, it's what you did growing up in our neighborhood," recalled Waitkus's younger sister, Stella Kasperwicz. "There was this park behind our house where everything centered, and Eddie loved playing ball there."

Young and in love with baseball, Waitkus's dominion was Cambridge Field, a neighborhood park just one block from his home at 281 Portland Street. East Cambridge was working class, a place where values and responsibilities were learned early in life, and Cambridge Field was an oasis of green in the middle of an industrial landscape known as the "Detroit of the East." Eddie Waitkus's first fling with baseball took place at Cambridge Field, where he learned to play the game bare-handed. He threw right-handed naturally and loved to pitch, but catching the ball without a glove was the hard part. According to his father, baseball was a "silly sport," and because money wasn't abundant in the Waitkus household, a baseball glove had to wait. But when his son was eight, Stephen Waitkus, a butcher by trade, came home from work one day and presented Eddie with a gift—a first baseman's mitt. The elder Waitkus was an accomplished swimmer, but he knew nothing about baseball. Young Eddie was thrilled with the glove. He didn't have the heart to tell his dad that he was actually a pitcher and that the glove was for the wrong hand. Instead he went out to Cambridge Field that evening and started to teach himself to throw left-handed. "I can remember the day daddy bought me the glove just as if it were yesterday," Waitkus said years later. "I loved that glove. I took it to bed with me, slept with it under the pillow, and took it to school. I still have it. It wore out and I had it patched. It must have been to the shoemaker's at least ten times. I'm going to save the glove to give to my boy if I ever have one."

As a youngster, Eddie Waitkus watched the moves of the older ballplayers, especially the first basemen. He studied the way they glided into position for a throw, legs spread and the base behind their feet, not between them. Jack Burns was one of those first basemen a young Waitkus studied at Cambridge Field. Burns played seven years for the St. Louis Browns, ending his major league career in 1936, as Waitkus prepared for his senior year in high school. Burns took the rawboned youngster under his wing and taught him the finer points of fielding. For hours each day, Waitkus was there, learning. One day, he knew, he'd be out there in the sunlight.

Waitkus and his sister, Stella, were raised in a close, church-going family. On Sundays they attended St. Patrick's, and although Stephen Waitkus worked long hours at the Faneuil Hall market in Boston, and Eddie played baseball daily in a park district league throughout the summer, the family gathered together for dinner almost every evening. The depression years often made decisions for families, and in 1933, when Waitkus was fourteen, his mother, Veronica, was hospitalized with pneumonia. She died days later. Her death was a devastating shock, and it marked the first turning point in Waitkus's life. "If mother hadn't died, Eddie would have gone to college, and his life would have been different," said Kasperwicz. "He was always a happy person, so sure of himself. People liked him because he had a very pleasant way about him, very easy going. He was my older brother, and I idolized him."

Waitkus, gifted as an athlete and student, began to shape his destiny at Cambridge High and Latin School, where he studied foreign languages as an honor student, was a star debater, and graduated sixth in a class of six hundred. In April 1936, a school publication, *CHLS Spot-Lite,* wrote: "Eddie Waitkus can't seem to keep off the Honor Roll." One spring afternoon in Waitkus's sophomore year, with his first baseman's mitt tucked under his arm, a teenage Eddie Waitkus walked onto the high school baseball diamond during a team practice. "I have a first baseman, son," said Sonny Foley, Latin's coach.

"Just let me take a few grounders, coach," Waitkus pleaded.

For the next several minutes, Foley watched Waitkus gracefully and flawlessly scoop up grounder after grounder. Foley hit each ball harder and harder, but each time Waitkus came up cleanly with the ball and fired a strike back to the catcher. When Foley had seen enough, he told the kid to grab a bat. When Waitkus drove line drives to every corner of Russell Field, Foley knew he had himself a new first baseman.

Waitkus was a legend by the time he left Cambridge Latin. As a senior in 1937, his heroic feats included a .600 batting average and a prodigious home run at his high school park. The towering blast sailed over the right-field fence at Russell Field and landed on the roof of a "three-decker," the name given to apartment houses that line most East Cambridge streets. "Eddie Waitkus, to the delight of Cambridge fans and the despair of his rivals, smacks them into the bleachers with that willow stick of his," wrote the *Cambridge Review,* Waitkus's high school yearbook. Named to every All Scholastic team of greater Boston in 1937, he seriously considered an offer to play college ball at Holy Cross. "I hesitated before turning down the Holy Cross bid," Waitkus said. "But I wanted to make baseball my career. I figured the sooner I got started the better off I would be." Instead of going to college, Waitkus played in the Suburban Twilight League of Boston, run by Ralph Wheeler, the prep editor of the Boston Herald. Wheeler was a huge Chicago Cubs fan, and he had a strong connection with the National League club, acting as an unofficial scout for the Boston area. Waitkus played for the Frisoli team in the Suburban League. The following year, Waitkus was selected to play in the "vacation league," comprised of teams representing various summer resorts in Maine and New Hampshire. Wheeler strongly urged Waitkus to play in the Maine League because it offered the best semi-professional competition in New England.

Waitkus signed with the Worumbo Indians of Lisbon Falls, Maine. In 1938, he became the hottest baseball commodity in New England, and he experienced his first taste of star treatment while playing for the Lisbon Falls club. On a warm night in late August, the entire town of Lisbon Falls held a celebration for the Indians after they captured the Maine championship and won two games in a national semipro tournament in Wichita, Kansas. "With the fire department turning out, with sirens cranking, with automobile horns honking and with the local drum corps adding to the reception with martial music, Lisbon Falls turned out en masse this evening to welcome its team back from the Kansas wars," the local newspaper, *The Press Herald,* reported.

Waitkus had a great tournament in Kansas. He hit over .500 and played perfectly at first base. A board of major league scouts named him to an all

America semipro team after his outstanding play. In Boston, sportswriter Fred Barry unwittingly penned Waitkus's destiny: "These big league 'wise men' viewed the left-handed batting and throwing of 19-year-old Waitkus and termed him a 'natural.'"

Ralph Wheeler did not lose sight of Waitkus. "There was no way Ralph was going to let Eddie get away," said Lennie Merullo, a Boston area native and former Chicago Cubs shortstop, who was directed to the National League club via Wheeler. A close friend of Cubs' chief scout Clarence Rowland, Wheeler arranged for the Cubs to get a close look at Waitkus when they made their last trip to Boston to play the Bees at National League Field. Waitkus donned a Cubs uniform and worked out with the team before the Cubs-Bees game. Gabby Hartnett, the Chicago manager, said Waitkus showed "great promise" at first plate and at the plate.

The Chicago Cubs went on to lose the 1938 World Series in four straight games to New York, but they beat the Yankees in the bidding war for Waitkus. Just before Christmas, the Cubs gave him a $2,500 bonus and signed him to a contract to play for the Moline Plow Boys of the Three-I League—for $300 a month. "The first thing Eddie did when he signed his Cubs' contract was buy me a pair of ice skates," said Waitkus's sister, Stella. "It was such a wonderful Christmas that year."

Waitkus epitomized grace at first base. His six-foot frame comfortably carried a rugged 175 pounds, and his ability to stretch for wild throws gave him "can't miss" status. But it took a few weeks for his power and speed to take hold. At Moline, Waitkus played his first games under the lights, and that took some adjustment. He hit .189 for the first eight weeks. Once used to seeing the ball at night, Waitkus started to hit in bunches. Waitkus was named to the 1939 Three-I League All Star team, along with center fielder Barney Olsen, a Boston area player and a protégé of Wheeler. His .330 average led the league, and the Cubs moved him up to the Texas League the following year. "I guess I just needed to get used to being an Owl Leaguer," Waitkus said.

At Tulsa, where there was much better pitching, Waitkus hit .320 for the Oilers and led the circuit in stolen bases. In June, the Cubs, quite concerned about the failing right arm of Dizzy Dean, decided to option him to Tulsa. The Cubs hoped a few months in the hot sun of the Texas League would help Dean's tired arm. Dean spent two months with the Oilers, and when the team was on the road, he roomed with Waitkus. The legendary pitcher struck up a quick friendship with Waitkus and his Boston-area pals on the club, Olsen and Merullo. On the surface, it appeared to be an accident waiting to happen: Waitkus, a young, well-spoken New Englander, fluent in Lithuanian, Polish and German, with promising baseball years ahead of him; Dean, native of Lucas, Arkansas, ringleader of baseball's infamous Gas House Gang, and murderer of the English language. But they became good friends, and Dean was one of Waitkus's early supporters.

One morning when the Oilers were in Fort Worth for a Texas League road game, Dean decided to take his three new friends to visit his farm in nearby Garland. "We all piled in Dizzy's new 1940 Ford "Woody" station wagon," recalled Merullo. "On the way to Garland, where Diz had his farm, we stopped at a small air strip in the middle of nowhere. 'Come on, fellas, we're all gonna go for a ride,' he said to us. Before we knew it, Diz was introducing us to a friend of his who owned a biplane at the airstrip, and we each took turns riding in the plane. That's the way Dizzy was—he knew everybody. When we finally got to his farm, we were really surprised because his house had practically no furniture in it. But there was this one room filled with scrapbooks and scrapbooks of newspaper clipping of Dizzy's career. Eddie, Barney, and I spent most of the day reading those old newspaper stories about Dizzy."

In 1941, the Cubs invited Waitkus to Catalina Island for spring training. Dean was quick to sing the praises of Waitkus to all the right people. He told Chicago columnist Warren Brown: "There is the best young ballplayer at any Major League camp this spring. I've seen him play enough at Tulsa to know what he can do. There ain't going to be anybody in the National League outfield him." Dean knew exactly what he was saying. Waitkus sailed off the island a member of the Chicago Cubs; he was one of three rookies in Chicago's opening-day lineup.

Waitkus made his major league debut on April 15 at a cold and windy Wrigley Field. Batting second, he singled in four trips to the plate and played flawlessly at first base, recording thirteen putouts as the Cubs beat the Pirates 7–4. The Cubs and Waitkus struggled during the first month of the season. After the opener, the team went into a horrible batting slump, and by early May the Cubs found themselves in last place. Waitkus played in twelve games, nine as a starter, and collected five hits, all singles, in twenty-eight trips to the plate. In the middle of May, the Cubs optioned Waitkus back to Tulsa. When he returned to the Oilers, Waitkus refused to sign the standard players contract until two provisions were added: first, that his roommate would be second baseman Don Johnson and second, that he would no longer be referred to as "junior" among the players, as he was affectionately called during the 1940 season. "Don was older than us, he had a family, and he was a real gentleman," said Merullo. "Eddie and Don got along great, and it was good for Eddie to be around a veteran like Don. As for the 'junior,' Eddie was always so young looking, I guess the nickname fit him. He was very slender, had practically no beard, and always looked like he was sixteen. He probably didn't care too much for 'junior.' Maybe that's another reason he wanted to room with a veteran like Don."

After spending the rest of the season at Tulsa, where he batted .300, the Cubs promoted Waitkus in 1942 to the Los Angeles Angels in the Pacific Coast League. "It's always been the contention of those who follow the Texas League that if a fellow can hit around .300 down there, he can come pretty close to doing it in the big league," said Waitkus. "One reason is, there isn't any rabbit in the ball they use in the Texas League, which is not true of other minor leagues where they use balls that must be loaded with dynamite the way they explode when smacked with the bat." Waitkus battled .336, tops in the Pacific Coast League for everyday players. He led the league with 235 hits, finished second in total bases, including 40 doubles, and was considered the finest major league prospect in the minors for 1942. Veteran Angels manager Arnold Statz said of Waitkus: "Nothing upsets him. Nothing bothers him. What's more, he's a great team man, always keeps the rest of the gang pepped up when the going is hardest." And coach Bill Sweeney said, "Having been a first baseman, I just marvel at the youngster. He makes every play smoothly and easily. My eyes have been glued to him since spring training and they're still glued on him. I haven't found a fault in his play yet."

Waitkus also enjoyed the many perks associated with being a baseball star in Los Angeles.

The Pride of the Yankees was filmed while he was with the Angels, and the producers selected Waitkus for several baseball action scenes at first base and at the plate. (Apparently his swing was more believable than Gary Cooper's.) And then there was Lupe Velez. The voluptuous movie star watched batting practice at an Angels game one afternoon with some of the players' wives and reportedly asked, "What does that handsome youth do with his spare time?" She asked to be introduced to Waitkus and, in front of everyone, gave the blushing bachelor a passionate kiss. "Cambridge Ed Waitkus Scores a Hit with Lupe," Waitkus's hometown newspaper reported.

The Angels led the Pacific Coast League for most of the season, but they blew a four-game lead to Sacramento in the final five days to finish in second place. "And first baseman Eddie Waitkus," the *Los Angeles Times* reported, "just a week ago chosen the club's most valuable performer, batted in nary a run all week, obviously being preoccupied with his imminent military service." Indeed, although Waitkus was ready to move up to the Cubs for the 1943 season, World War II had other plans for him.

Instead of joining the Cubs, Waitkus was drafted into the army and spent the spring of 1943 in basic training at Fort Devens, Massachusetts, where he prepared for his overseas assignment as a member of the 544th Engineer Boat and Shore Regiment. A letter he sent to Cubs general manager Jim Gallagher reflects Waitkus's sense of duty and spirit:

> Just a few lines to let you know how things are going. I'm stationed here for my basic training. It's a comparatively new branch but one of the best. Our job is "to get there first with the most men and sweep the beaches clear," as our song goes.
>
> We're a picked group, men with athletic background and fairly high marks in mechanical aptitude tests. It's a tough outfit, but I couldn't stand one of those soft desk jobs. Isn't that just like a left-hander? I should be here for a while.
>
> Gosh, I hope baseball goes on. I think I'd go rattraps without any scores to look for. You'd be surprised at the number of men who follow the sport here in the barracks.
>
> I'm sorry I won't be with you this spring, but it's something that can't be helped. A lot of other guys are giving up something, too. I guess what we're fighting for is to make a world where a lot of little guys named Joe won't have to leave home and a future anywhere on the face of the earth.
>
> Wow! I mustn't start getting philosophical!
>
> Anyway it's been swell being affiliated with you, and I hope this mess is over soon, so we can take up where we left off. Good luck to you this season and keep them playing.

On May 2, 1944, Eddie Waitkus, a member of the weapons section of Company D, 544th Engineer Boat and Shore Regiment, left the Port of San Francisco on the USAT *Sea Devil* and passed under the Golden Gate Bridge for overseas duty. Twenty-two days later, he debarked at a place called Oro Bay, New Guinea. For the next seventeen months, Waitkus participated in amphibious assault missions in the Pacific, securing beachheads for General Douglas MacArthur's "Operation Cartwheel," which cut off Japan from its Southeast Asian Empire. From Oro Bay, he went with the first elements of the Fourth Engineer Special Brigade to Maffin Bay, Dutch New Guinea, and after a brief preparation period, he joined the large task force and landed with D-Day assault units on the Japanese-held Island of Morotai, Netherlands East Indies, in September 1944.

From Morotai, Waitkus departed for Bougainville in the Solomon Islands to join the Thirty-seventh Infantry Division for combat operations. He was then assigned to the Fourteenth Corps of the Sixth Army for an amphibious assault on the island of Luzon. As the Cubs were winning the National League pennant in late September 1945, Waitkus and the 544th became the first American troops ashore at Wakayama, Japan.

His combat experience earned him ten meritorious service awards, including four Bronze Stars and four overseas bars. His awards and medals included the Bronze Arrowhead, the American Theatre Ribbon, the World War II Victory Medal, the Luzon Campaign Bronze Star, the Asiatic-Pacific Campaign Medal, the New Guinea Campaign Bronze Star, the Northern Solomons Campaign Bronze Star, and the Philippine Liberation Ribbon.

In Cooperstown, New York, there is no plaque in the Hall of Fame for Eddie Waitkus, but his Pacific adventure was noted in a special exhibit honoring the fiftieth anniversary of World War II. "War slowly reached out and gathered baseball into its deadly grasp. . . . By the end of the war, more than 400 players active in the Major Leagues missed at least an entire season because of wartime service." So read the brochure for the National Baseball of Fame and Museum exhibition, "Baseball Enlists," a tribute to major league ballplayers who fought in the war, as well as the game itself: "As the American military shipped out, bats and balls traveled with them. After the engineers built a loading dock or landing strip, they often built a baseball diamond."

The exhibit featured a note Waitkus sent to a friend in 1945, while he was stationed at the Port of Manila, supporting ground troops clearing the

Japanese from Luzon. Waitkus had just been placed on temporary duty with the special service office and put in charge of regimental athletics and recreation, a nice assignment after a long and dangerous Pacific campaign. In the note—to a friend named Jim—Waitkus wrote, "It was swell to play again, and we'll have plenty of baseball for a while at least."

6

Chicago to Philadelphia

On a clear, bright March morning in 1946, Eddie Waitkus relaxed against the batting cage at a sun-splashed baseball field on Catalina Island, site of the Chicago Cubs' spring training camp. He was twenty-six years old, and baseball was back in his life. The Cubs had invited him to spring training, and this time, he knew, his minor league days were behind him forever. Waitkus took in the California sun with ease and enjoyed the sights and sounds of baseball again. As he hummed a tune, which he always did when all was right with his world, and watched the players go through their drills, his quiet was suddenly broken.

"So we got a left-handed tenor for first base," said Charlie Grimm, manager of the Cubs, the defending National League champions. "Tell me, young man, do you also play the banjo?" "Jolly Cholly" Grimm, veteran of twenty major league seasons, was in his tenth year managing the Cubs. Grimm was a rotund, jovial man and a fan favorite in Chicago. He coached third base with a theatrical flair and loved to go jaw-to-jaw with the umpires. On a disputed call, he'd turn his hat askew and belly up to the ump, all the time his long arms waving in the air, Grimm's attempt to get the crowd going. He was a skillful first baseman during his playing days, but more importantly, Grimm considered himself an expert baritone and an even better banjo player.

"No, sir, not the banjo," Waitkus answered. "But I fool around a little with the mouth organ."

"Young man," Grimm continued, "I don't know whether to give you a tryout or an audition, but trot down to first base, and I will see how you handle low grounders—the high notes can wait."

For the next quarter hour, Grimm hit ground ball after ground ball at Waitkus, and, as he had done some eleven years earlier when Cambridge Latin coach Sonny Foley gave him the same test, Waitkus handled each ball perfectly. After hitting an especially wicked one-hopper at Waitkus, Grimm said, "Young man, if you can sing like you field, you're going to be a helluva first baseman."

Waitkus left Catalina Island a member of the Chicago Cubs' major league roster. "Sure, I used to think a lot about the Cubs and the fellows I played with and wondered if I'd ever get another chance to play with them," Waitkus said shortly after spring training. "There wasn't a ballplayer in the service who didn't think about getting back to the game and hoping he would have enough on the ball to get back his old job. But I felt right at home the first day of practice. Who knows? Maybe the army really builds men, like it says on the recruiting poster." Waitkus even owned a Cubs National League championship diamond ring, although he was in Japan when the Cubs were winning their pennant. Cubs owner P. K. Wrigley had the championship ring specially designed for his players—he was proud of his team. But he wasn't totally benevolent; the players had to purchase the rings.

Waitkus faced a tough time cracking the starting lineup, and the Cubs faced an even tougher task in repeating as National League champs. The Cubs won the pennant in 1945, before losing the World Series to the Detroit Tigers in seven games, but with fine major league talent still in the war service, baseball in 1945 remained below par. About the 1945 World Series, veteran Chicago baseball writer Warren Brown wrote:

"Baseball writers from all over the country were assembled at Detroit when the Cubs arrived to begin the 1945 world series. An Associated Press reporter made his rounds asking each individual writer which club he thought would win. When he approached a writer from Chicago, expecting to get the customary "Cubs" reply—such is civic pride—he was startled to be told: "I don't think either one of them can win it." That came close to being the best forecast made of that or any other world series.

"It went the full seven games before the Tigers took the odd contest and became world's champions. Long before that point was reached even the players themselves had given up trying to figure out what might happen next. Fly balls were dropping between fielders who made no effort to catch them. Players were tumbling going around the bases. The baseball was as far removed from previous major-league standards as was possible without its perpetrators having themselves arrested for obtaining money under false pretenses."

In 1946, Waitkus joined a Cubs team that included Tulsa pals Don Johnson and Lennie Merullo. Also on the club was veteran first baseman Phil Cavarretta, the 1945 National League batting champ (.355) and Most Valuable Player. Cavarretta also led all hitters in the World Series with a .423 average. Waitkus had a formidable task in front of him. As Chicago baseball writer Edgar Munzel explained to his readers: "Waitkus' chances for a regular job when the Cubs' spring camp was opened on Catalina Island looked about as promising as beating out Joe Stalin in a Russian election." The players, however, especially those who played with Waitkus in the minors, had little doubt about his chances to make the club. "There was no way Eddie wasn't going to make the big league roster," said Merullo. "The way he played in the tough Texas League and in the Pacific Coast League before going off to war—the Cubs were just waiting for him to get back home. It was a foregone conclusion, at least among the players, that he'd make our team. The only questions for Grimm was where to play Cavarretta."

Waitkus had some luck. Bill Nicholson, the Cubs' regular right fielder, who led the league in homers in 1943 and 1944, struggled through a horrible year in 1945, hitting an anemic .243 with just thirteen home runs. "The trouble with Nicholson," said Grimm, "is that he fell into a slump and listened to too much advice. It got so he was even listening to the fans." Nicholson was given a pay cut for the 1946 season, but his slump continued.

On April 25, as the Cubs opened a two-game series against the Cincinnati Reds at Wrigley Field, Grimm moved Nicholson to the bench and Cavarretta to the outfield. First base now belonged to Waitkus. Batting sixth in Grimm's lineup, Waitkus seized the opportunity. He singled twice, doubled, and drove home two runs in his first game as a starter. The Cubs committed three errors and lost 7–5, but Waitkus was on his way. By the middle of June, he was hitting .310 and playing perfectly at first base. "Waitkus, without a doubt, is the finest first baseman I've seen in a long time," said Grimm. His hitting also impressed the Cubs' manager. Waitkus's war years did little to ruin his timing at the plate. With his smooth, quiet, inside-out swing, Waitkus hit the ball with authority to all fields. "It was like his head actually rested on top of the bat," recalled Merullo. "His head never moved. He could wait on a ball, never move, and at the last second get his hands to flick the bat at the ball and poke it over the shortstop's head for a hit. I can still picture that swing in my mind."

On June 23, Waitkus's name entered the major league record books. The Cubs were playing the Giants at the Polo Grounds in a doubleheader, and in the fourth inning of the opener, Marv Rickert, also a rookie, and Waitkus hit back-to-back inside-the-park home runs, becoming the first major leaguers to accomplish such a feat. Waitkus never cooled off in 1946. He finished the year hitting .304, the only Cub regular to hit over .300. In 113 games, he collected 134 hits, including twenty-four doubles, five triples, four home runs, and fifty-five RBIs. The Chicago chapter of the Baseball Writers Association of America voted Waitkus Rookie of the Year. Waitkus received 230 points in the poll, easily outdistancing the runner-up, Del Ennis of the Phillies. Waitkus also placed thirteenth in the voting for National League Most Valuable Player, a rare honor for a rookie. He finished ahead of some big baseball names, including Johnny Mize of New York and Marty Marion of St. Louis.

In the off-seasons, Waitkus returned to his Boston-area home to live with his father and his sister, Stella. He looked up his East Cambridge school chums, always found time to visit with Frank Wheeler, and relaxed at the Lithuanian American Citizens Club of Cambridge. Waitkus enjoyed his Lithuanian heritage, and according to his friends, the only time he lost his temper was when someone good-naturedly called him a "Polack." "I'm Lithuanian, got it, Lithuanian, not Polish!" he'd say. Waitkus was also proud of his war service; he joined the East Cambridge V.F.W. Ferricane Post 3275 shortly after returning home.

When Waitkus signed his 1947 contract with the Cubs, Grimm said, "Waitkus is easily the best all-around first sacker in our league. Furthermore, he is just now beginning to develop as a ballplayer. Wait until he really gets settled up here." Waitkus, however, struggled through the first half of the season with more than his share of nagging injuries. In spring training, he nursed a sore elbow and knee following a collision with a wall near first base. He also missed twelve games in April because of a spike heel, but he returned at the end of the month to go two-for-four as the Cubs and rookie pitcher Doyle Lade beat the Dodgers 3–1. In late June, Waitkus was out of the lineup because of a bruised shoulder, and upon his return on the Fourth of July, he injured his ankle when he smashed into the Wrigley Field bricks chasing a foul ball.

Waitkus's early-season bumps and bruises did not affect his hitting too much—he was batting .306 in mid-May—but his usually brilliant fielding was hurting. On June 16, he made two errors at Wrigley Field which led to a 2–1 loss to the Dodgers. "Waitkus, who made only four errors last season, already has been charged with five bobbles this year," wrote Edgar Munzel of the *Chicago Sun*. The Cubs' record was 36–36 following the All Star break, when Waitkus returned to action nursing a sore ankle. After an eleven-day eastern road trip, the Cubs returned to Wrigley Field in early August in sixth place, fifteen and a half games behind first-place Brooklyn. More than thirty-four thousand fans watched a somewhat revitalized Cubs team tag seven Dodger pitchers for a 12–7 victory. Waitkus hit safely five times and scored four runs. And later that month, he hit his second career inside-the-park home run, this time with the bases loaded. Again, the round-tripper was hit in a doubleheader at the Polo Grounds in New York.

By mid-September, the Dodgers were running away with the 1947 National League pennant; the Cubs trailed Brooklyn by twenty-three and a half games. Almost every year since the end of World War II, the final few weeks of the baseball season die slowly each afternoon at Wrigley Field. The autumn breezes blow in from Lake Michigan; the loyal young Cubs fans who filled the park all summer long are back in school; and the Cubs, who usually have been mathematically eliminated from pennant contention, perform before a canvass of empty green seats. On September 15, 1947, Wrigley Field was a desolate place. Waitkus was battling a severe batting slump, but the onset of cool, fallish weather apparently was to his liking, or maybe it was the thought of next year's contract. Before a slim crowd of 3,966, he led the Cubs to a 3–2 win over the Boston Braves. "Eddie Waitkus finally shook off his long hitting slump yesterday with the recklessness of a lumberjack at a tree-chopping rodeo. His triple and two singles were the chief contribution to the Chicago offense," noted Milt Woodard of the *Chicago Sun*. With all the injuries during the first half of the season, Waitkus hit a respectable .292 and collected 150 hits in 130 games. Grimm's prediction that Waitkus was "just now beginning to develop as a ball player" was correct.

Waitkus, as Grimm suggested, quickly settled in as a ballplayer in Chicago. He was clearly one of the stars of the Cubs, usually batting second or third in the lineup behind fan favorites Stan Hack and Peanuts Lowrey. Waitkus had even beat out the popular Phil Cavarretta at first base. The Cubs—and the city of Chicago, with its sophisticated nightlife—were a perfect match for Waitkus. Because the Cubs played only day games at Wrigley Field, there was plenty of time for the players to explore the club circuit on the city's hustling North Side. "Eddie always liked the classy nightlife, even when we were kids in East Cambridge," remembered Frank Sharka. "Whenever we went out, especially when we had dates, he dressed up in a coat and tie and wanted to go to the fancy joints."

Waitkus became fast friends with two of the Cubs' fun-loving bachelors, Marv Rickert and Russ Meyer. Rickert was a six-foot-three bundle of energy who, like Waitkus, joined the Cubs in 1946 following three years of war service. His teammates called him "Twitch." Meyer, who had an explosive temper on and off the field, loved the ladies and spent much of his free time in pursuit. The "Mad Monk" would marry five times. Waitkus, Rickert, and Meyer made the rounds as a threesome in postwar Chicago. Waitkus was blond and lean, and he carried a small scar above his right eye, a memento from a Cambridge High and Latin hockey game. He was the quiet one of the group, but he had an enviable savoir faire with the ladies. He soon became a favorite of the young female fans at Wrigley Field. The Eddie Waitkus fan club was one of the most popular in Chicago, and the young girls, who made up most of the membership, waited after each and every home game outside the players' exit at Wrigley Field to get a close-up look at their new idol. Waitkus, according to his teammates, was also popular with the girls off the field. "Ed wasn't a woman chaser," said Meyer, "but the women loved him. He talked the talk in a real classy way. Ed always looked great, usually a double-breasted suit with some kind of flower in the lapel. The guy loved to look good. I loved women, but Ed really connected with them."

Waitkus, Rickert, and Meyer lived in the Sheridan Plaza Hotel, not far from Wrigley Field. After most games, they'd meet in the bar of the hotel before heading off for a night on the town. During one particular cocktail hour, Meyer was quietly entertaining a couple of lady friends at a secluded corner booth when he suddenly bolted from the table, his nose covered with blood. "We never really got all the details," said Merullo, who was sitting with a couple of teammates not far from Meyer. "All of a sudden, Russ jumped up, blood gushing from his face. One of the gals apparently took offense to something Russ said—or did—and bit his nose, took a real hunk of skin right off. With Russ, you never knew what might happen." Waitkus, according to Merullo, observed the fracas from his solitary position at the end of the bar, scotch-and-soda in one hand, a cigarette in the other.

Most evenings were not as exciting. After a cold beer at the Sheridan Plaza bar, Waitkus and some of the players took dinner at Tony's Italian restaurant on Lawrence Avenue and then made their way to Helsings for some bowling. The 5100 Club was also a favorite late-night hangout of Waitkus and his pals. Comedian Danny Thomas, a close friend of outfielder Peanuts Lowrey, made sure the Cubs had ringside tickets available to them when he performed at the 5100 Club. "We enjoyed each other's company back then," said outfielder Andy Pafko. "Players spent a lot of time together. We traveled on trains, played cards, and talked baseball. We really got to know each other. The ballplayers were different than they are now."

The atmosphere surrounding the Cubs was pretty relaxed. Charlie Grimm was very likable as a person and as a manager. A group of writers always followed him around, in hotel lobbies and in the clubhouse; Grimm loved the attention and the writers loved Grimm. As defending National League champions, the 1946 Cubs had a bit of a swagger to them. Although he was a rookie, Waitkus fit right in. "When Eddie trotted out to first base, you could tell he had something special," said teammate Bill Nicholson. "He had a great, quiet confidence about him, and it showed in the little things, like when he took warm-up throws between innings. He really had a comfortable style."

The Chicago clubhouse was usually very lose. Grimm played the banjo, Waitkus sang in the shower, and Rickert loved playing the role of team clown. "Any time you needed a laugh, you found Rickert," said Merullo. "He loved to crack you up. One of his favorite gags was to walk around the locker room in nothing but his jock strap. He'd pull up both straps around his shoulders and parade around the room. Now here was a guy who was way over six feet tall. It looked pretty ridiculous, but it kept us all loose. Marv was one of Eddie's closest pals, and he really enjoyed Rickert's clowning-around. Eddie was always considered somewhat urbane, especially for a baseball player, but he always enjoyed a good laugh, and he hung around with the guys who would always provide him with one—guys like Rickert and Meyer."

In 1948, his last year with the Cubs, Waitkus batted safely 166 times, and although he continued to play an excellent first base, Grimm, with no explanation, sent him to the outfield for twenty games late in the season. He hit for a .295 average and played in the All Star game at Sportsman's Park in St. Louis. The Nationals lost 5–2, and Waitkus walked in his only appearance at the plate, pinch-hitting for Johnny Sain in the sixth inning. Since joining the Cubs after the war, Waitkus was one of the brightest stars on a team that was going backwards. Following their 1945 pennant, the Cubs finished third the next year but some fourteen and a half games back of league-leading St. Louis. In 1947, the Cubs dropped to sixth place, twenty-five games back of Brooklyn, and in 1948, they hit the cellar, a woeful twenty-seven and a half games out of first place. When the winter baseball meetings convened in Chicago in mid-December 1948, the Cubs were looking to make a deal that would stop their skid. Waitkus, their best defensive player and most consistent hitter, became a hot item at the baseball meetings.

The Chicago Cubs weren't the only team in the National League looking to turn their fortunes around via the trade route. The year 1949 was to be a renaissance of sorts for the Philadelphia Phillies. In 1943, the franchise was in financial shambles. The National League took control and sold the team to a group headed by William Cox, described as a New York sportsman. But Cox had trouble from the start—with his team and with league president Ford Frick. Cox had a gambling problem, notably betting on the Phillies. Frick launched an investigation, and in late November, Cox was banned from baseball. His controlling share of the team—worth $400,000—was sold to Philadelphia businessman Robert M. Carpenter. Carpenter, who received moral support from the Philadelphia Athletics' Connie Mack, named his son, Robert Carpenter Jr., who was just twenty-eight years old, president of the club.

The young boss of the Phillies began a slow but steady rebuilding process. And at the major league meetings in December 1948, he made headlines with a blockbuster trade. He brought Waitkus to the Phillies, along with pitcher Hank Borowy, for Dutch Leonard, the Phillies' ace right-hander, and Walt Dubiel, also a pitcher. Rogers Hornsby, a former Cubs manager, couldn't believe the Cubs traded Waitkus, a favorite in Chicago. "The Cubs have two real ballplayers—Andy Pafko and Eddie Waitkus," Hornsby said. "They can't trade the best first baseman in the business."

Waitkus was at the Melrose, Massachusetts, home he shared with his father, sister, and brother-in-law when he heard he was traded. That same day, he received two congratulatory telegrams from Russ Meyer and Bill Nicholson, whom the Cubs had sent to the Phillies in different deals following the 1948 season. Waitkus was surprised he was sent to the Phillies because published reports had him headed to New York or Brooklyn. But he was happy to join up again with Meyer and Nicholson in Philadelphia. "I'm willing to wager that Russ will win a lot of games for [Phillies manager] Eddie Sawyer," Waitkus said upon learning of his trade to Philadelphia. "He's really got good stuff. As far as Nick, watch him go now that he's away from Wrigley Field." Waitkus, however, was quick to let everyone know that he was not a disgruntled ex-Cub. "The day I returned home from the service I found a registered letter containing a check for $1,000 with a note from Cubs general manager Jim Gallagher saying, 'this may come in handy.' There's not many guys like that. Take it from me, he's made of the right stuff. Chicago was a grand place to play. The only thing that bothered me was the shirts in center field made a tough background for hitters."

Baseball experts agreed, Bob Carpenter had pulled off a gem of a trade. He not only out-foxed the cagey veterans at Chicago, Grimm and Gallagher, but he bested the New York Giants and Brooklyn's Branch Rickey. The Giants and their new manager for 1949, Leo Durocher, were interested in acquiring Waitkus, as was Durocher's old team, the Dodgers. Brooklyn had wanted Waitkus badly, so much so they reportedly came to the meetings ready to give the Cubs five players for Waitkus. But neither Durocher nor Rickey ever had a chance to make an official offer to the Cubs because Carpenter managed to get to Grimm and Gallagher first.

In one of the first interviews with the Philadelphia press, Waitkus told reporter Frank Yeutter he was surprised at the trade: "I was happy enough over there. And I thought I was playing pretty fair baseball. But the worst of it was you never know what position you'd play. I never played anything but first base, but one day Grimm handed me a football helmet and said, 'You're an outfielder.' So I played right field for more than a month, and how I escaped lethal injuries I'll never explain."

The transition to Philadelphia was made easy for Waitkus because two of his closest friends from the Cubs had also found their way to Philadelphia a few months before him. "The first thing I thought of, when it dawned on me that I was a member of the Phils, was my two pals, Bill Nicholson and Russ Meyer," said Waitkus. "It will seem like old times playing with

Nick and Russ." Waitkus wasted little time in endearing himself to Phillie fans and his new teammates. In a pre-season game at Shibe Park, the Phillies' home field, he belted a two-run home run to beat the cross-town Athletics 4–2. Waitkus received a huge ovation, and the Phils stormed out of the dugout to greet him at home plate. "You might have thought Eddie Waitkus won a World Series game when he hit a home run over the right field wall in the seventh inning yesterday," *The Sunday Bulletin* reported. He carried that momentum right into the 1949 season. By the first week in May, Waitkus, batting third in Eddie Sawyer's lineup, was hitting .308 and stinging the ball to all fields. And his play at first base was outstanding. He was also becoming a team leader. When Bill Nicholson struggled with an awful batting slump, he went to Waitkus between games of a doubleheader with Cincinnati and confided, "Every time I go to the plate, I have a half-dozen thoughts go through my mind, and I end up popping the ball up." Waitkus told him, "You're not paid to think. You're paid to hit the ball." Nicholson drove home five runs in the nightcap as the Phillies beat the Reds 8–1.

Throughout May and June, the Phillies battled to stay above .500, but Waitkus was making a lasting impression in Philadelphia. His teammates called him "the Fred Astaire of first basemen," and his manager compared his fielding with players such as Joe Kuhel and George Sisler. One Philadelphia newspaper ran a feature story on Waitkus's glove and included the headline, "He Can Make the Hard Plays with Any Glove." Waitkus was also making his mark at the plate. A few days before he was shot at the Edgewater Beach Hotel, in an eighteen-inning game against the Pirates, he singled, doubled, and tripled twice to lead his team to a 4–3 victory. Waitkus roomed with his pal Nicholson and enjoyed the Philadelphia nightlife with Meyer. It seemed as though nothing had changed from his days in Chicago—he was on top of his game and enjoying his life off the field. "Eddie was a young, happy ballplayer with everything going for him," said his sister, Stella. Just prior to that fateful trip to Chicago, where his life intersected with Ruth Ann Steinhagen, Waitkus was playing the best baseball of his entire life.

A happy-go-lucky minor leaguer, Waitkus hit .336 for the Los Angeles Angels in 1942, tops in the Pacific Coast League. Courtesy of the Boston Public Library, Print Department.

A member of the army's 544th Engineer Boat and Shore Regiment, Waitkus saw fierce fighting in the Pacific during World War II. His combat experience earned him ten meritorious service awards, including four Bronze Stars. Courtesy of the Boston Public Library, Print Department.

Waitkus and fellow Boston-area native Lennie Merullo pose together at Braves Field in 1946. The Boston Braves honored the young war hero with a special Eddie Waitkus Night. Courtesy of the Boston Public Library, Print Department.

Waitkus, shown here in the winter of 1946, was a handsome, highly intelligent bachelor who loved the opera, spoke four languages, and took great pride in his dress, often wearing cashmere sport coats and double-breasted suits. Courtesy of the Boston Public Library, Print Department.

Waitkus slides home safely as a member of the Chicago Cubs. When the Cubs traded Waitkus to the Phillies in December 1948, Rogers Hornsby said, "They can't trade the best first baseman in the business." Author's collection.

On the shores of Lake Michigan, the Edgewater Beach Hotel was considered the finest resort hotel in the city. On June 14, 1949, in a room on the twelfth floor, Ruth Ann Steinhagen shot Waitkus. Photographer: Hedrich-Blessing. HB-23718-C. Chicago Historical Society.

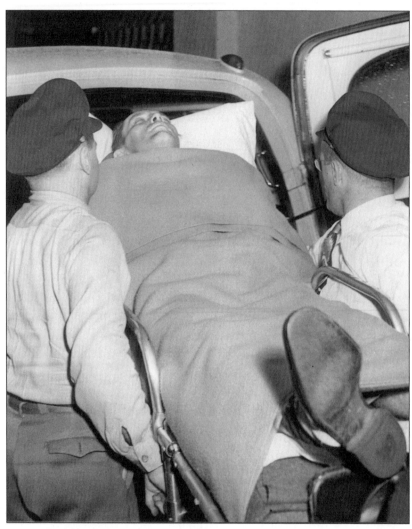

Waitkus is loaded into an ambulance outside the Edgewater Beach Hotel after the shooting. The bullet pierced a lung and lodged near the spine. When Waitkus arrived at the hospital emergency room, he was bleeding internally but conscious. Doug Meyer Collection.

Steinhagen confers with her parents, Walter *(left)* and Edith *(right)*, prior to her hearing in felony court on charges of assault with intent to kill. Deputy bailiff Jennie DuBray is in the background. Doug Meyer Collection.

On June 30, 1949, Steinhagen has her day in court. A packed felony courtroom in Chicago watches as state's attorney John Boyle *(right)* admonishes her; Waitkus sits in a wheelchair and stares ahead. AP/Wide World Photos.

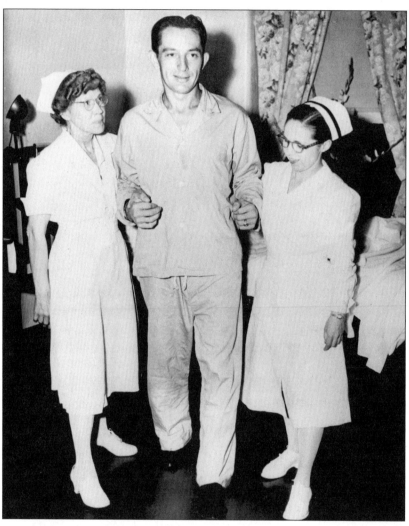

Waitkus is helped by nurses at Illinois Masonic Hospital, where he spent a month recovering from his gunshot wound. He received more than three thousand cards, letters, and telegrams from well-wishers. On his left hand he wears the 1945 Chicago Cubs National League championship ring. AP/Wide World Photos.

Waitkus, pictured with Stan Lopata *(left)*, Russ Meyer *(right)*, and two batboys, enjoys a visit to the Phillies' clubhouse during the summer of 1949. His teammates were shocked to see how much weight he had lost. AP/Wide World Photos.

Russ Meyer *(left)*, Frank Wiechec *(center)*, and Waitkus work out at Athletic Field in Clearwater, Florida, in the winter of 1950. Wiechec, the Phillies' trainer, supervised a rugged daily training program for Waitkus. Author's Collection.

Waitkus wed Carol Webel on November 17, 1951, at St. Patrick's Roman Catholic Church in Albany, New York, the bride's hometown. The couple had met in Clearwater Beach, Florida, the year before. Author's Collection.

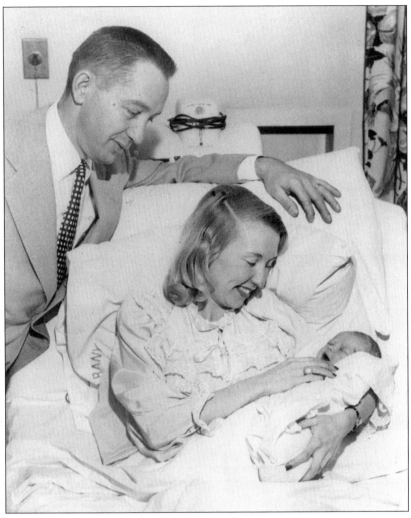

Waitkus looks on in February 1953 as his wife, Carol, holds their new baby, Veronica, named after Waitkus's mother. The couple's second child, Ted, was born in 1956. Author's Collection.

Waitkus, a silky-smooth first baseman, fielded .993 for his entire career and posted a perfect fielding percentage of 1.000 during the 1954 season. National Baseball Hall of Fame Library. Cooperstown, N.Y.

7

Baseball Annies

The Waitkus shooting put a national spotlight on the huge number of teenage girls throughout major league cities who spent much of their summers chasing their baseball heroes. A *Time* magazine reporter who interviewed Waitkus while he was still in the hospital wrote: "He sat up in bed and tolerantly described Ruth as a 'Baseball Annie,' one of an army of hero-worshiping teen-age girls who follow players around." The press quickly picked up on Waitkus's description of Steinhagen as a "Baseball Annie" and used it in headlines throughout the country. Teenage girls have always followed baseball players around, and throughout history the athletes have always had their own special names for these girls, including "Baseball Sadie" and "Chicago Shirley." Steinhagen, however, was vastly different from these girls who congregated outside the clubhouse doors. If she had actually made contact with Waitkus, either by directly asking him for his autograph or merely talking with him, one psychiatrist theorized, she would not have gone through with the shooting. Instead, she quietly allowed her wild dream to become a reality, changing her life and Waitkus's forever.

Writing for the *Sporting News* in May 1950, Philadelphia baseball reporter Stan Baumgartner attempted to profile these young, female fans. "The modern 'Baseball Sadie,'" wrote Baumgartner, "is much more dangerous, bold, sex-conscious than her prototype of 20 or 30 years ago. Many come from the 'best' of families. They have good educations, dress in the latest fashions, make up conservatively, and can take their place in any gathering.

"They form fan clubs, have meetings and ask their favorites to attend. Their loyalty sometimes reaches a dangerous stage. They go after their man with a determined recklessness—whether he is single or married—that has forced baseball clubs, including the Phillies, to take steps for the protection of their players. At the request of the Phillies' players, much of their correspondence is 'screened' for crank notes—letters from adolescent girls and older women who have only one motive in mind, to meet and have dates. If one of the letters seem worthy of the investigation by the police, it is turned over to the authorities. In other cases they may be forwarded to the parents of the girls who wrote them."

Baumgartner then went on to actually categorize "these Baseball Sadies: (1) Young teen-agers who have crushes and idolize the players. (2) Older women who want to get married. (3) Women who are looking for a payoff."

The "Baseball Sadie" story, according to the editors of the *Sporting News,* "stirred up a hornets' nest of angry feminine fans." Kay Shaw wrote the newspaper: "I don't think Branch Rickey is going to like my cancellation of a season ticket. The reason: I don't want to be tagged a Baseball Sadie. I'm a decent, clean-cut girl who likes baseball for what it is and not for meeting ball players."

The Waitkus shooting received tremendous newspaper coverage in major league cities and prompted clubs to take a hard look at player security. During an August road trip to Cincinnati in 1950, the Phillies' Richie Ashburn became the object of an overzealous teenage girl. At the request—or demand—of manager Eddie Sawyer, management at the Phils' hotel—the Netherland Plaza—placed a special guard to protect Ashburn and his teammates.

The girl, according to published reports, said she saved up money to travel to Crosley Field to watch the Phillies. She bought a box seat behind the Philadelphia dugout and tried to get Ashburn to come out to talk with her. She became so bothersome that the Phillies' traveling secretary, Frank Powell, threatened to get the police if the girl didn't stop annoying his players. That night, at the Netherland Plaza, she patrolled the lobby demanding to see Ashburn. Nothing ever happened, and the girl was escorted out of the hotel.

Sawyer was a huge critic of young female fans, baseball's version of the teenage bobby-soxers. "It's bad all around the circuit," he complained, "But it's worse in Brooklyn and Chicago than anywhere else. They don't want autographs. They have hundreds of them. They just use that as an excuse to talk with the players."

Chicago was "the badlands of bobby-sox fans," Waitkus told *Sport* magazine a few months after the shooting. "Always has been. About 90 percent of the wildly enthusiastic autograph seekers are teen-age girls. They get to the park before the ball teams, which arrive at about eleven in the morning. The ticket windows aren't open, but the bobby-soxers are there. And if you try to ignore them—wow! There is only one way to enter or leave the park for players. The girls know they have two strikes on you because of their sex and they take advantage of it. Nothing much you can do about it, either. Until what happened to me last summer, I never thought too much about it, but now I'll admit I am sort of jittery about my first meeting with the bobby-sox crowd in Chicago."

Baseball fan clubs were gaining popularity across the country after World War II, and membership was comprised mostly of teenage girls. Fan clubs were big in Chicago, and the three most active clubs were for Bill Nicholson, Hank Borowy, and Waitkus before they were traded to Philadelphia. Many of the major league teams helped form women's clubs, to help educate female fans about such things as the vocabulary of the game and strategy. But fan clubs were usually small, private groups that had no ties to the major league teams. Members received monthly newsletters, which usually included photos, poems, and stories about their favorite player. Steinhagen, according to her conversations with authorities following her arrest, never admitted to belonging to the Eddie Waitkus fan club.

Sawyer, who was always irritated by girls hanging around his players, had his personal view of the way to protect his athletes from overzealous fans: "I'd like to see the day come when players can drive into ball parks through underground tunnels and get out the same way." Major league players were protected by the baseball clubs inside the parks, but they were on their own outside. Most clubs, however, furnished "player only" parking lots near the clubhouse exits, and it was common practice for teams not to furnish casual telephone callers with any personal information about players.

Seventeen years before the Edgewater Beach shooting, another Chicago Cubs star was shot by a lovesick girl. In July 1932, shortstop Billy Jurges was shot twice by Violet Popovich Valli, a local cabaret girl, at the Hotel Carlos, near Wrigley Field. The girl, who told hotel officials, "he turned me down," forced her way in Jurges's room and took a handgun from her purse. In a violent struggle for the pistol, three shots were fired. One bullet struck Jurges in his right side, ricocheted off a rib and came out his right shoulder. He also suffered a flesh wound on the little finger of his right hand. The girl was also hit in her right hand. Like Waitkus, Jurges was remarkably lucky. The attending physician, also at Illinois Masonic Hospital, said the bullet that traveled through the right side of Jurges's chest caused no damage to any vital organ, and no bones were broken in his hand.

Police discovered a suicide letter in the girl's hotel room. Addressed to Valli's brother, the handwritten note blamed Cubs' star Kiki Cuyler and another one of Jurges's friends for breaking up her love affair: "To me life without Billy isn't worth living, but why should I leave this life alone. I'm going to take Billy with me."

Valli was charged with assault with intent to kill. But Jurges told the court he did not want to prosecute, and the judge dismissed the case. But he added, "let's hope that no more ball players are shot." Jurges recovered quickly and rejoined the pennant-winning Cubs, and Violet returned to the cabaret circuit.

Ruth Ann Steinhagen and Violet Popovich Valli will be remembered forever in the dark side of baseball history as two overzealous, aggressive female fans. The truth is, though, that baseball, especially in its early years, desperately needed and coveted female fans. Turn-of-the-century baseball had a rough and rowdy reputation. Baseball grew in the cities, and it was a game for roughnecks who were boisterous and drank too much, not a sport that beckoned high society. Self-control—by the players and the fans—was a huge issue, and local clergy and press denounced the rowdyism. The games had a cock-fight mentality to them as brawls broke out on the field and in the stands. In his book *Playing For Keeps—A History of Early Baseball,* Warren Goldstein explained the role of the female fan:

"Baseball clubs and promoters wanted women at games as evidence of the game's popularity. Many spectators would be drawn by the legitimacy that only women could confer on the game. Most important, however, women were supposed to help men control themselves on the ballfield. Like the umpires (and like their supporters among the press), women personified standards of behavior that could, theoretically, keep men's behavior within certain boundaries. . . . Women, in the familiar Victorian scheme, were to domesticate the ballfield."

To this point, club owners devised a special day for women to attend games. *The Baseball Timeline, the Day-to-Day History of Baseball, from Val-*

ley Forge to the Present Day, explains that Ladies Day started in Cincinnati in 1876: "Noting that attendance is up—with many women in the crowd—whenever handsome Tony Mullane pitches, the Cincinnati owner schedules him to throw every Tuesday at League Park and designates it as 'Ladies Day,' beginning a long baseball tradition." (That misty Tuesday afternoon—June 14, 1949—was Ladies Day at Wrigley Field.)

As baseball's modern era began in 1900, the game was still very rough. It was played mostly by streetwise toughs who reveled in what was called the "inside game"—where the outcome usually was determined on the base paths. It was a brutal contest of well-timed and well-placed base hits, sliding with spikes up, and plenty of verbal abuse; it was the game of John McGraw, Ty Cobb, and the Baltimore chop. And women were loving it. So much so that "Take Me Out to the Ball Game," written in 1909, paid homage to the female fan of the era:

> Katie Casey was baseball mad
> Had the fever and had it bad.

Women fans continued to watch major league baseball games with great enthusiasm throughout the twentieth century. In 1909, *Baseball Magazine* published a less-than-flattering poem entitled "Female Fan": "She shrieks and she squeals at base hits and steals . . . but takes the next morning's paper to see which team has won." But in 1949, that same publication had formed quite a different opinion of female baseball fans. "There was a time," wrote Jim Crusinberry, "when a man never took his wife—or his girl friend—to a ball game. As far as baseball was concerned, her place was in the home. Today, her place is in a choice box seat. There was a time when the wife or girl friend would remark on how good a pitcher was because he could pitch the ball where the batter could hit it every time. But when something like that is happening today, the wife or girl friend is the first to yell, 'take him out.' Yes, women fans have taken their place in baseball. Their patronage is important. Without that patronage the game would not have reached its present success."

As long as there is baseball there will be Baseball Annies. But the Annie of the twenty-first century is more subtle. Former San Francisco Giants catcher Brian Johnson described the phenomenon this way: "These women still exist, but they're more camouflaged nowadays. It's a risky situation—the accusation is always on the front page, the retraction is on the back."

Shortly after the Waitkus shooting, *Baseball Magazine* called female baseball fans "hero worshipers." But it added: "There probably are more than ten million enthusiastic women baseball fans in the United States, and Eddie Waitkus had to meet the one among them who proved to be dangerous."

8

Clearwater Beach

Sitting up in his hospital bed, the now honorary member of the 1949 National League All Star team groaned as he listened to the radio broadcast from Ebbets Field.

"Something always happens to the Nationals in these games," Eddie Waitkus told a visitor. "They always pull something you won't do in high school."

Waitkus, who was leading in voting for first base when he was shot, was named to an honorary position by National League manager Billy Southworth. The game, which the Americans won 11–7 to take a commanding 12–4 lead in All Star victories, was a comedy of errors for Waitkus's team. The Nationals made five errors, more than any other All Star team. A United Press report of the game asked: "Would it had been different if Eddie was there?"

In the opening inning, Cardinals rookie Eddie Kazak threw wildly to the Giants' Johnny Mize at first. The ball bounced out of Mize's glove, and that miscue eventually led to four unearned runs.

"The error was charged to Kazak but the consensus among the seasoned observers who saw this 16th annual classic was that any good first base sacker—and particularly Waitkus, of the Phils—would have had the ball in his apple-hand," the U.P. reported.

By the time of the All Star game, Waitkus's physical condition was steadily improving, and one week before he was transferred across town to Billings Hospital on Chicago's South Side, Waitkus felt strong enough to talk to the entire Phillies squad—twenty-seven players and coaches—via telephone.

Wanting to show his teammates he was indeed in fine spirits, Waitkus relied on his New England wit. He joked that he had just heard from Chicago police that Steinhagen had confessed she had also planned to shoot Cy Perkins, the Phillies' fifty-five-year-old coach.

"She said Cy is number two on her hit parade," Waitkus told his audience. Perkins was not amused. "If he thinks that's funny, it's not," he said.

On a Friday night in July, two weeks after Waitkus talked with his teammates, doctors discovered a low-grade infection in Waitkus's lung. They again drained fluid from his chest cavity, and early the next morning, Waitkus underwent surgery to remove the bullet. Removal was necessary because the bullet had moved from outside the chest cavity near the spine to inside the chest cavity where it was causing the infection.

In August, the Associated Press ran a story saying the Hall of Fame had written Waitkus asking for the bullet. The report, carried in newspapers across the country, said the museum in Cooperstown, New York, planned to make the bullet a permanent exhibit. "Not true," Tim Wiles of the Hall of Fame said years later. "Nobody from here ever asked for the bullet."

On July 17, one month after he walked into Ruth Ann Steinhagen's room, Waitkus left Billings Hospital. His plans, he told reporters at the hospital, included getting some rest in Philadelphia and then visiting family in Melrose, near Boston. "What about the bullet," someone asked, apparently needing some final closure to Waitkus's bizarre episode in Chicago. "Do you have it?"

"No," he said, "I haven't got the bullet. I think the doctor kept it."

Eddie Waitkus stepped off the TWA Stratoliner to a hero's welcome at Philadelphia's international airport. His baseball career had been interrupted by three years of war, and he had survived and returned to the top of his game. But his world had changed again, this time in a Chicago hotel room. Now, with five hundred cheering admirers standing in a steady rain, Waitkus began yet another recovery. Thin and looking pale, he carried a drain tube in his back, the result of the latest surgery. "I don't know when I'll be able to play again," he told his fans. "I only hope I can play well when I come back." Physically and psychologically, he had to find a way to return to excellence. Everyone—the Phillies, his fans, Eddie Waitkus himself—expected it.

At least his sense of humor was always there for Waitkus, especially in tough moments. Exhausted and wanting to end the barrage of questions from reporters and fans on a positive note, he told everyone about a get-well card he received from former teammate Peanuts Lowrey, the ballplayer Ruth Steinhagen had first admired. "Peanuts told me, 'I'm glad you came along, handsome.'" Waitkus's psychological journey to recovery actually began when he arrived in Philadelphia. The doctors in Chicago had done their job. Now it was up to Waitkus to overcome his fears of the future.

"It wasn't so bad at first in the hospital," he confided to Taylor Spink of the *Sporting News*. "The doctors keep you so doped up that you live in sort of a dream world, where you float from one happy cloud to another, never able to concentrate on anything that may worry you.

"You get so much attention, have so many visitors, there is so much going on you live in a busy world of your own where there is no time to think for any length of time about your own problems. There are always others worse off than you are.

"It is only when you begin to convalesce in earnest that fears assail you. I think my first big moment of uncertainly came shortly after Dr. Will Adams had removed the bullet. To remove the bullet it was necessary for him to cut in deep, spread a muscle, slice here and there.

"I know that if anything had happened to the muscles in my back I was through playing ball. No one said anything after the operation. I wondered—were they afraid to tell me? I watched their faces, not daring to ask. The nurses were too attentive, it seemed. Did they feel sorry for me?

"I had to know. I couldn't put it off any longer. When Dr. Adams came in I said, 'Well, Doc, what's the verdict?' It seemed an eternity before the Doc smiled and tapped me softly on the shoulder. 'You'll be as good as ever.' He assured me. 'Maybe you'll be able to get on a uniform and play before the season is over.'

"Then he explained that I would have to keep a tube in my back so that the wound would heal from inside out, pushing the infection before it. 'It ought to clear up in two weeks and we can take out the tube,' he said.

"But the wound did not clear up in two weeks. They finally sent me back to Philadelphia, where I took an apartment by myself and waited and waited. That was really when it got tough. After the excitement and company of the hospital that apartment seemed like a dungeon.

"The tube in my back made it almost impossible for me to sleep without pills, and those left me groggy. I awakened two or three times at night with nothing to do but think.

"I began to wonder all over again. Did the doctors know their business? Were they letting me down easy? Wouldn't my back ever heal?

"In the mornings I was so tired I didn't feel as I could put one foot out of bed. It was often too much of an effort to go after my meals—but I knew going out after meals and mixing with people was something the doctors wanted me to do.

"But I couldn't gain weight. Then the fans gave me a great night in Philadelphia. I felt proud until I looked at my picture. Was I as bad as that? Was that skinny sunken-cheeked guy me? I don't think I slept a wink for a week and I didn't look in the mirror. I was sure I wasn't ever going to play ball again.

"My liberation came the day they took the tube out of my back, told me I was okay. That night I think I slept the clock around. I wasn't worried about getting well any more.

"But then I began to fret about whether the long layoff would affect my batting eye, whether I would be able to move about first base as I had before I was shot."

In early August, while Waitkus recovered, the Phillies were mired in their worst slump of the 1949 season. Losers of five games in a row, ten of their last thirteen, the Phils were getting ready for a game with the Pirates when an unannounced visitor walked into their Forbes Field clubhouse. "How about winning a ball game," Eddie Waitkus asked his teammates, who were playing under .500 ball since he was shot.

Bored with convalescing in his Philadelphia apartment, Waitkus, accompanied by Babe Alexander of the Phillies' front office, had boarded an airplane to Pittsburgh to boost his team's morale. As always, Waitkus's dress was immaculate. He wore a gray suit, starched blue shirt, and a multicolored tie decorated with a hand-painted pheasant. He told his teammates he was feeling fine and that he had actually gained back ten of the fifteen pounds he lost following the surgery to remove the bullet. The surprise visit, it appeared, was not only aimed at raising the spirits of the slumping Phillies, but it was also designed to let everyone know that Eddie Waitkus was well on his way to recovery.

Seeing their first baseman did help the Phils—they beat the Pirates—

but no one was convinced Waitkus had regained his health. "He looked like a skeleton, nothing but skin and bones," said Andy Seminick. "It shook us all up." In a conversation later that summer with Eddie Sawyer, Waitkus said: "The last five weeks were the most rugged that I've spent in my life. If I had to go through it again I almost feel like saying it would have been better if she hadn't missed."

Less than two weeks after he visited his teammates at Forbes Field, Waitkus was again the center of attention. On August 19, Shibe Park was in a festive mood, decorated in red-white-and-blue bunting and "Welcome, Eddie Waitkus" signs. Although he did not play, Waitkus wore his Phillies uniform for the first time since the shooting. He looked frail, however, and the large wool jersey hung on him.

He was greeted by a standing ovation from nearly twenty thousand fans and received a bounty of gifts: a new Dodge convertible, a television set, two radios, golf clubs, luggage, wrist watches, a movie camera, a full wardrobe—including at least ten suits—a $500 savings bond, a two-week vacation at an Atlantic City hotel, and a honorary membership in the Veterans of Foreign Wars. The gift-giving was preceded by an elaborate program featuring a variety of music by a local string band, a drum-and-bugle corps, and a blind lyric soprano who sang "Because" and "Kiss in the Park." A father-and-son team concluded the festivities with a selection of cowboy songs.

Dick Sisler, the man who had replaced Waitkus at first base, presented the team gift. Standing at home plate, Waitkus fought back tears as he accepted a bronzed first baseman's mitt and two silver baseballs mounted on a velvet-covered plaque. Below the glove, a silver plate carried the etched signatures of Bob Carpenter, Babe Alexander, Eddie Sawyer, trainer Frank Wiechec, all the players and coaches, and the Philadelphia baseball writers who covered the team.

"You put me on the spot on June 14, so I hope you have a speedy recovery and come back and take the job away from me," Sisler said as he handed the gift to Waitkus. At the end of the ceremony, his voice cracking with emotion, Waitkus stepped up to the microphone to thank everyone. "I don't know what the future holds for me," he said, "but you have given me something I will always remember."

The Phillies were beginning to play solid baseball when Waitkus was shot, but the club went through a horrible July swoon. They lost five games in a row and ten out of thirteen at one stretch. Waitkus's absence from the lineup was hurting the Phillies. From mid-June until early August, the club played under .500 baseball. Dick Sisler did a fine job filling in for Waitkus at the plate, hitting .274 with eleven home runs and fifty-four runs batted in. But Sisler couldn't match Waitkus's grace at first base. Knowing Sisler had limited range at first, the Phillies' infielders were more deliberate with their throws. Such conservative fielding allowed many base runners to beat out infield hits. "With Waitkus at first," said Sawyer, "the guys could get the ball and let loose, knowing Eddie would come up with any wild throw." In mid-August, Sawyer had had enough. He held a closed-door clubhouse meeting and read his ballplayers the riot act, threatening jobs if play didn't improve. The Phillies responded positively and ended the year in third place, their best finish since 1917. Russ Meyer and Ken Heintzelman each won seventeen games, while Robin Roberts carded fifteen victories.

Baseball loyalty, however, isn't always what it appears, and Carpenter had his own plans for Waitkus for the 1950 season. Sisler played well during the last half of the 1949 season, and Carpenter wanted to know as soon as possible who his starting first baseman for the 1950 season would be. In November, with permission from baseball commissioner Happy Chandler, Carpenter sent Waitkus to Clearwater Beach, Florida, site of the Phillies' spring training camp. March 1 was the spring training start date in 1950, so the commissioner needed to make an exception for Waitkus.

Carpenter also sent the Phillies' trainer, Frank Wiechec, to Clearwater Beach, with orders to get Waitkus in the best possible shape by the time the rest of the team arrived for spring training in March. Wiechec, a Temple University graduate, was considered to be ahead of his time in physical conditioning. His goal: build up Waitkus's strength and endurance and increase his lung capacity as quickly as possible. Wiechec also had a reputation for being tough. "Frank probably pushed Waitkus to his limit," said Jack Rockwell, a former athletic trainer and retired executive director of the National Athletic Trainers Association. "Frank's programs were much stronger and advanced than most trainers back then. He was way ahead of his time. Most trainers did not have a great background in physiology and anatomy, but Frank did."

Wiechec supervised a daily training program for Waitkus—runs along the beach, bicycling, hours of calisthenics, resistive exercises, massages to break up the adhesions and scar tissues, and plenty of boat rowing to get the back muscles in shape. The wounded athlete told his teammates that the Clearwater Beach experience was, "the four most horrible months in my life. Worse than anything in the army, worse than New Guinea or any place in the Philippines."

For the first time in his life, Waitkus had doubts about himself, about his ability. His outlook on life was veiled, according to his close friend, Russ Meyer: "Ed was always a loosey-goosey guy," said Meyer. "But after the shooting incident in Chicago, Ed was never the same." Spring training had always been a relaxed time for a genuine star like Eddie Waitkus, but his winter training going into 1950 was different. Although his Clearwater Beach stay was first-cabin—a furnished apartment on the beach, a car and chauffeur, even a fishing boat, supplied free of charge by local Clearwater businesses—Waitkus had to learn to be alone with his fears.

"The loneliness was part of it," he later told *Sport Life* magazine. "The pain was part of it, but it went deeper than that. There was an awful doubt in my mind—or at least in the back of my mind. And no matter how I'd try to ignore it—-always knew it was there. I kept up with the program Frank and the doctors mapped out, but then at night, sitting alone in my room, those doubts would pop up again. Somehow it didn't seem possible I'd ever be strong enough to play nine innings of baseball. Frank's encouragement did an awful lot for me—and that's about all I had. The days seemed to drag at Clearwater and when the rest of the gang finally showed up, including my roommate Bill Nicholson, why it was like finding all your long-lost friends."

Frank Wiechec's tough training and the bright Florida sun were paying off for Waitkus. His stamina increased daily, and he began to get his color back as he ran the beach among the Clearwater tourists. The pavilion was the meeting spot for all the Clearwater Beach regulars, especially the vacationers who stayed at the beach for extended periods. Waitkus enjoyed the socializing. By nature, he was an extrovert, in a quiet, confident sort of way. His gentle demeanor was complemented by a soft and charming Boston accent. His friends agreed—Waitkus never enjoyed being the show, but he did love being around it. He usually stopped by the pavilion after his morning runs. There was B. J., a three-year-old girl who Waitkus befriended, and her family; Ed, an actor who called Waitkus years later when he got a bit part in the movie *On the Waterfront;* and Mary, confined to a wheelchair, who received much of Waitkus's attention. They became his friends, people who could fill up the lonely days, if not the nights.

And there was Carol Webel, a pretty, twenty-year-old blond girl from Albany, New York. Carol, who vacationed with her family each winter at Clearwater Beach, first noticed Waitkus as he took his morning runs. She was a regular at the pavilion, and she and Waitkus became friends almost immediately. They walked the beach together in the afternoons when Waitkus was finished with Wiechec's workouts, and they enjoyed quiet dinners together in the evenings. And they promised to keep in touch once their Clearwater Beach experience was over. Carol, Waitkus told friends years later, gave him the inspiration to recover physically and mentally. "Eddie was witty, smooth, and very friendly on the beach," Carol Webel remembered decades later. "He was sensitive, fun, and a joy to be with."

"Waitkus was a bachelor at the time [of the shooting], and nobody ever enjoyed life more," Phillies teammate Richie Asburn said of Waitkus. "He was young, handsome, successful in baseball and went first class all the way. He was always the perfect gentleman, impeccable in manners and dress. He sometimes seemed like an intruder, out of place in the brawling, tough world of baseball. Eddie was a ladies' man, and I emphasize the word ladies. He didn't get involved with the "Baseball Annies" and the camp followers. He went first class and that included his lady friends."

Carol Webel was such a lady.

9

Comeback

A combination of father confessor and Simon Legree"—that's how Eddie Waitkus described Frank Wiechec during their winter at Clearwater Beach. Papa Wiechec, as Waitkus called him, was much more to the injured ballplayer than just a physical therapist and trainer. When Waitkus struggled and became depressed, it was Wiechec who listened with a sympathetic ear. "Frank felt the wrath of all my worries and my pent up fears," said Waitkus. "I don't think he ever took a drink before in his life, but he went along with me for a beer every night and we talked like buddies in the army used to talk."

Wiechec was a perfect match for Waitkus. He was young and intelligent—with bachelor's and master's degrees in education from Temple University—and he had the confidence of everyone in the Phillies organization. "Frank was the closest thing to a doctor we had on the team," said Maje McDonnell, the Phillies' batting practice pitcher. McDonnell was correct in his analysis of Wiechec, who left a teaching job at Temple late in 1948 to join the Phillies. Wiechec had spent four years as a supervisor and instructor of physical therapy at the Mayo Clinic. He brought a scientific approach to training baseball players. Trainers in the past had used an assortment of liniment, oil of wintergreen, and rubbing alcohol to treat the myriad of ailments major league ballplayers faced during the long season.

Wiechec possessed the knowledge to stop problems before they became worse. If he thought an injury might bring on future complications, he called for an X-ray at once; if a player complained of a sore throat, Wiechec had a thermometer in his mouth; bruises and sore arms were iced down immediately to help prevent blood clots.

Eddie Sawyer had complete trust in Wiechec. If a player wasn't 100 percent and Wiechec thought he shouldn't play, he stayed on the bench. Late in the 1949 season, when the Phillies rallied to finish third, it was Wiechec who took on the role of disciplinarian. Because he enjoyed universal respect from the players, Wiechec was given duties beyond that of most trainers. Sawyer ordered him to keep tabs on the players during road trips. Wiechec was in charge of bed checks and morning reports; he even handed out the meal money. On his professional resume, Wiechec listed "helping the Phillies earn third place in 1949" as his most outstanding performance.

Wiechec always thought baseball teams were archaic in their thinking regarding physical conditioning. Years after he left baseball, Wiechec told an athletic trainers association conference: "It takes only six hours for muscles to tighten, so imagine what condition baseball players' muscles must be in after laying off all winter. Before a baseball player ever picks up a ball at spring training, he should be studied. Then before throwing and running, there is a course in isometrics, isotonics, and general muscle toning that stretches and strengthens the muscles that are below par.

"But do you think baseball people will listen? Oh, no. The first thing they do is throw baseballs, swing bats, and run. Some players put on two and three sweatshirts and rubber shirts, run in the outfield when someone is looking or merely stand in the sun to sweat off winter weight. Nothing could be more damaging to muscles and useless as training. Sweating off weight that way actually weakens they muscles they are going to use."

Getting Waitkus in top shape was Wiechec's first major challenge as Phillies trainer. Bob Carpenter kept a close watch on his efforts and ordered Wiechec to furnish him with regular progress reports. In a letter written to Philadelphia sportswriter Stan Baumgartner, Waitkus gave a vivid account of life with Papa Wiechec:

> Dear Stan:
> If you only knew how sore I feel, you would realize that I had to shackle myself to the desk to write this letter. Therefore, any resemblance between this and a logical letter is purely coincidental.
> Clearwater is still Clearwater. But Frank Wiechec is playing Simon Legree with this Topsy better than any fictional character, and doing the job with a wicked snap of the whip. You know how conscientious he is! Well, that conscientiousness has been doubled in spades. Thank goodness Sunday comes once a week. It is the

only day I get away from the constant bending and pavement pounding that would make a debutante's reducing routine look like a simple game of Tiddly-Winks. To be serious, Stan, it really gets rough once in a while. Florida is swell—when the wind is howling and the shutters are snapping. Those are the days I can't get out to Wiechec's mangler.

I gave up smoking the first of the year and the alcoholic output is strictly the cold brew before dinner. Saturday night I have the brew after dinner, too.

I'm rounding into pretty good condition. I've thrown and played "pepper" and the reflexes are all they ever were. When the aches get real bad, I just give myself a pep talk and remind myself that I'm still too young to go to work.

Russ [Meyer, right-handed pitcher who was spending his honeymoon in Clearwater] started working out with us today. We gave him the works. Bet Mrs. Meyer doesn't let him out tomorrow.

Do you know, I believe that guy Wiechec stays awake nights dreaming up exercises, but they do put muscles where there was none before.

He was afraid my back might bother me, but all I have out of it is a pain in the neck—a real pain, I mean. But I'll be ready for the gang when they get down—and I'll do the shooting this time at first base.

With best wishes to all the fans and thank them for their confidence and kindness.

Sincerely, Ed

A late winter snow fell on Philadelphia as the Phillies boarded their private Pullmans at the Baltimore and Ohio Railroad station on February 26 for the trip to Florida and spring training. Absent, however, were Russ Meyer and Bill Nicholson, Waitkus's two closest pals who had already joined him in Clearwater Beach in January.

"Eddie, Russ, and Bill were a trio, always together," remembered Mary Meyer Oswalt, Russ's former wife. "They had such a good time together, even that winter when Eddie was trying to get back into shape after the shooting. Eddie had such a great sense of humor. His humor is what saved him, what got him through. He was a lovable, huggable kind of guy who never gave you the impression that was ever upset about anything. He was good looking, but his personality, humor, and charm is what captured you. He called all women 'funny honeys.' He adored women and was very good with them."

Meyer, who was called "Mad Monk" because of his temper, threw batting practice every day so Waitkus could work on his timing before the first intrasquad game. Waitkus repeatedly hit Meyer's favorite screwball. "I hit it so hard he got mad and threw his glove at me," Waitkus said.

Happy Chandler, when told about the workouts, fired off a letter to the Phillies. "Since official spring training cannot start until March 1," the commissioner wrote, "Meyer must stop throwing." But the unflappable Meyer used the reprimand to spin some positive public relations for Waitkus, himself, and the Phillies. "He's in great shape and was hitting the ball good," Meyer said. "As for me, I was ready to go nine innings when we had to quit. If our club gets off with the rest of the league, instead of having to come from behind in August, we'll win the pennant."

Waitkus enjoyed his successful mini–spring training with Nicholson and Meyer, but was he ready to step into a major league lineup? The Phillies had given Waitkus an opportunity to regain his strength and skills, but manager Eddie Sawyer wasn't about to blindly hand him a starting position. "Waitkus has to win his job back before he replaces Dick Sisler," Sawyer told everyone when he arrived at camp. "It was Dick's much improved all-around play that enabled us to pass the Boston Braves near the finish of the season and take third place in the National League. Sentiment can play no part in this highly competitive business." Referring to golfer Ben Hogan's miraculous escape from death in February 1949 after a speeding bus had slammed into his car on a small Texas Bridge, Sawyer continued: "You don't see Sammy Snead handing Ben Hogan any tournament victories. And certainly I am not going to put Sisler on the bench because Waitkus is well again." Internal injuries had nearly killed Hogan at the crash site, but he recovered to make a remarkable comeback in 1950, winning the U.S. Open. Like Hogan, Eddie Waitkus and the Phillies were poised to embark on their own miracle comeback.

After four months of brutal physical training—"four nightmare months," Waitkus called it—he now had to prove himself again. It wasn't just good enough to get into shape; he had to regain his baseball skills. "I feel good and strong," he said. "And my timing is better than it ever was. If I were the kind of hitter who has to wind up from Port Arthur, I might be worried. Then I might pull one of those muscles I had to work on so hard to get back into shape. But my style of hitting shouldn't put too much strain on my back while I'm getting competitive again."

Sawyer was intent on making 1950 a fresh start for the Phillies. Although the team came together late in 1949 to take third, Sawyer wanted some changes. He let his players know they had to win their jobs at spring training. Sawyer also made some new rules: Wives and children were not allowed to accompany players to camp; the entire team had to stay at the same hotel; and everyone walked the one-mile trek to Athletic Field together. He also wanted a new look. Gone were the old blue pinstripes, blue hats, and blue socks. "It reminds everyone of the losing thirties," Sawyer said. The Phillies' unofficial nickname—"Blue Jays"—was also retired. The new-look Phillies would wear home whites with bold red pinstripes, accented by red caps and socks.

By the time his teammates arrived in Clearwater Beach, the sun-baked Waitkus cut a fine figure in his Phillies uniform. His weight was back up to 170 pounds, and the bright Florida sun complemented his crew-cut blond hair and hazel-blue eyes.

Waitkus was a member of coach Dusty Cooke's team in the Phillies' first intrasquad game at Athletic Field, and he was greeted with a surprise when he approached the plate for his first at bat. The players on coach Benny Bengough's squad took a step out of their dugout and collectively "shot" Waitkus with toy pistols that fired a cork on the end of a string. Everyone enjoyed a good laugh, and Waitkus told the story for years.

In the game, Waitkus smashed three hits in three plate appearances; a line-drive double traveled all the way to the right-field foul pole. He also sparkled on the field, turning a tricky 3-6-3 (first-to-short-to-first) double play. Sisler, playing for the Bengoughs, collected two hits but had trouble at first. He failed to reach an easy pop foul and dropped a throw from third.

A few days later, against the Reds, Waitkus drove home three runs with a double and a home run; again he played magnificently at first base. In a game with the Senators, Waitkus hit two more doubles, and he tripled against the Red Sox.

Midway through the exhibition schedule, sportswriter Frank Graham found Sawyer during batting practice before a game at Clearwater and fished for information: "There was a story in the paper the other day that there was a contest at first base between Waitkus and Sisler." Sawyer admitted, "there was, for a while. But it's no longer a contest. Sisler hits a longer ball, but, day-in-and-day-out, Waitkus is the better hitter. And there isn't anything he can't do around first base. I just had to be convinced that after all he had gone through—not only the physical hurts, but the shock as well—that he had completely recovered before I made up my mind he was the one to play regularly. I've been convinced."

Bob Carpenter's decision to send Waitkus and Wiechec to Clearwater had saved Waitkus's career. Wiechec's grueling routine had strengthened Waitkus's muscles and given him the confidence to concentrate on his baseball skills. He once again moved comfortably at first base, dipped low for ground balls, and stretched his entire body for wild throws without much pain. Physically, he was positioned to start the 1950 season. Mentally, he knew, the road to recovery would be much tougher. The romantics say the baseball season enjoys a calm rhythm, but the players know baseball has always been a game for survivors. The long season—154 games in 1950—is played in spring's bitter cold and summer's oppressive heat; night games follow day games, followed by a string of August and September doubleheaders; and for most ballplayers, there looms the knowledge that there's always someone, either at the end of the bench or in the minors, who is a phone call away from taking away their jobs.

Waitkus's mental state was positive after spring training. He showed everyone, including himself, he was back on his game. What he needed to do was carry this attitude with him for the next six months, an entire baseball season.

10

Kankakee State Hospital

Once you drive past the tree-lined entrance, the circular paths seem to curl quietly through the hundreds of old oak, pine, and walnut trees. Dotted among this sea of green stand the many cottages of rough-cut limestone. The Kankakee State Hospital for the mentally insane presents a tranquil, bucolic landscape. Its post–Civil War architecture bespeaks a Midwestern college campus, not an insane asylum.

In the years immediately following World War II, the population at the hospital soared as many families turned to the state to care for their mentally ill family members. The hospital's 250 acres warehoused nearly five thousand mentally ill patients—"M-I's" the staff called them. Each crowded ward was lined with sixty to seventy beds, and the central dining halls, where the residents gathered in mass, were filled with rows and rows of long wooden tables. No one had separate living quarters.

Kankakee State Hospital was built originally to accommodate the "cottage system," a strategy developed in the late nineteenth century, where the mentally insane were cared for in small, homelike buildings scattered throughout the grounds. Patients who functioned well worked the farm and watched over the cattle. They tended to the garden and orchard, washed the laundry, sewed the hospital staff's uniforms, and wove their own rugs. It was here, in the turn-of-the-century environment, that Ruth Ann Steinhagen began her struggle to come to grips with her life after shooting Eddie Waitkus.

In the 1950s, despite the overcrowding, the culture and organizational structure at state mental hospitals had changed little from the 1890s. The society at Kankakee State Hospital resembled that of a "company town." Virtually all the staff—doctors, nurses, administrators, attendants, and laborers—lived on the hospital grounds. "From a sociological sense, all the state hospitals were the same back then," said Bill Briska, a published authority and researcher on the history of mental health care in Illinois. "In a sense, it was like going to college in the Midwest. No matter which college you attended, the experience was basically the same."

Much of the staff at Kankakee State Hospital came to the hospital from small, rural towns in southern Illinois. Whole families were recruited, especially after the war when the population increased dramatically. With the prospect of good housing on the hospital's campus and three free meals a day, the appeal was hard to resist for many. Because most of the employees and their families lived on site, there was a warm, benevolent feel to the hospital's society. Kankakee State Hospital scheduled a very active social environment for the patients: movies, dances, and concerts in the auditorium; church services on Sundays; seasonal festivities and pageants; picnics in the walnut grove; and liberal visitation policies.

When she arrived at the hospital, Ruth Ann Steinhagen, like every new patient, was first taken to a nineteenth-century brick-and-stone building featuring a clock tower that rose seven stories and overlooked the Kankakee River. The huge tower separated the building's two wings; male patients occupied one wing, female patients the other. New patients spent several weeks at the hospital's diagnostic unit, where they were treated and evaluated as to their functioning ability. The wards in the diagnostic unit were small, three or four to a room, and each patient received personal attention from the staff. The hospital's goal was to sort out the individuals into two broad groups: those who could be treated within a few weeks and released into society and those who needed long term care.

The patient population at Kankakee State Hospital in 1949 included individuals who suffered from a variety of illnesses. A large percentage were geriatric, whose symptoms of mental illness were really a manifestation of dementia, Alzheimer's, stroke, and arteriosclerosis. "Today, these people would be in nursing homes, not mental institutions," explained Briska. There was also a steady flow of people with acute mental disorders; they stayed a few months and were released. A small percentage of the population included mentally retarded patients and some individuals who suffered from substance abuse, usually alcoholism. Typically, patients came from

Chicago, Cook County, and its tier counties; like Steinhagen, many arrived from the court system or jail. It was in this population mix that Steinhagen attempted to regain her sanity.

Following the diagnostic phase, patients were categorized into three functioning levels. Higher-level patients, who were able to think in an organized manner, enjoyed a trusted position. They helped out the staff with various ward chores, such as changing beds and mopping floors, and their wards were not overcrowded. Living conditions for mid- and lower-level patients were quite different. The dormitories were overcrowded, with little or no room for personal belongings. The wards were filled with aggressive and untidy patients who needed much supervision. Lower-level wards were plagued with chronic, daily problems, such as broken windows, soiled linens, and an extremely high level of noise.

During her two and a half years at the hospital, Steinhagen, according to superintendent Dr. Ernest Klein, underwent electroconvulsive therapy to alter the chemical balance in her brain. In the early 1950s, patients usually received electroshock treatments without sedatives or anesthesia. The patient lay on a hospital gurney, and the doctor used a large clamp, with two electrodes on its ends, to administer the procedure. The clamp was fitted around the head, with the electrodes squeezed against the temples. A doctor then pushed a toggle switch on a small wooden box, releasing a small burst of electric current. The ensuing seizure caused the patient's arms and legs to shake uncontrollably for about a minute as the electricity passed through the head. The theory of electroshock treatment is that something in the seizure process affects the neurotransmitters in the brain. The exact cause-and-effect relationship is not entirely understood, but it was felt by most researchers at that time that the treatment helped to reorder the balance of neurotransmitters. The theory was that when the transmitters had fallen out of balance, symptoms of mental illness, such as schizophrenia, occurred. Today, with many different types drugs suitable to treat such complex illnesses and disorders, electroshock treatments now seem primitive and uncertain, if not harmful, to mentally ill patients.

Hydrotherapy and occupational therapy were the other two major treatment modalities Steinhagen experienced at Kankakee State Hospital. In an attempt to calm patients, various techniques of hydrotherapy, such as warm sheet packs, were used as sedative measures. Occupational therapy attempted to keep patients busy and engaged, in the belief that work was healthy.

Patients, depending on their functioning level, worked in various jobs throughout the hospital grounds. They performed small duties in the kitchen and in the dining rooms, and they worked outside on the farm and in the orchard, as well as tending to the hospital's greenhouse. Steinhagen was exposed to all this, and anticipating her release, said she might return to the hospital to work as an occupational therapist. "Patients identified with the staff involved in their occupational therapy," said Briska. "In a sense, it's like kids in school who say they want to grow up to be teachers."

Although Steinhagen had paranoid trends, doctors said, she was a very organized person. Her mother told doctors that her daughter had read several books on psychiatry in an attempt to analyze her feelings about Waitkus. Her elaborate plan to kill Waitkus was extremely methodical: She had avoided the need for a gun permit by purchasing a used rifle from a pawn shop; she had written a well-crafted note to lure Waitkus to her room; and she had used the name Burns, perhaps knowing the name meant something to Waitkus. Steinhagen also entered Kankakee State Hospital in a very organized state of mind. "Some schizophrenics show obvious craziness," said one psychiatrist. "She didn't. She was peculiar, guarded, but not bizarre. She was a quiet psychotic."

Perhaps that was the reason those close to her said they were surprised by her violent act. Although she used the middle name Ann, she was born Ruth Catherine Steinhagen, on December 23, 1929, in Cicero, Illinois. She attended public school and at one time was given a double promotion. Steinhagen spent two years at Chicago's Waller High, and she earned her degree from Jones Commercial High School. She said her life's ambition was to become a secretary. When she shot Waitkus, she was employed at the Continental Casualty Company in downtown Chicago. Her mother said, "Ruth wouldn't hurt a fly," but she admitted her daughter once told her she was going to get a gun to kill Waitkus. A Continental Casualty official said she was a good worker and never gave a sign she was emotionally upset.

Possessing an organized mind probably helped Steinhagen adapt to life in the insane asylum. Being able to process new information allowed her to be less fearful and less overwhelmed. "It most likely made her amenable to the therapeutic opportunities that were available to her," said Briska. Steinhagen's attorney, Michael Brodkin, said she became adept at occupational therapy at the hospital. The daily work filled her days and kept her mind active. It also provided Steinhagen with an opportunity to show hospital officials that she could accept and hold responsibilities, get along with others, and follow authority. These traits were not merely virtues, but they measured her progress and helped build a case for discharge.

As Waitkus started his long fight to regain his health and his career, Steinhagen apparently found solace and help in her battle with schizophrenia in the controlled environment at Kankakee State Hospital. A very young woman, Steinhagen's delicate journey to recovery began at Kankakee, but her struggle to maintain a normal existence continued throughout her entire life, long after her release from the hospital. Waitkus's road to recovery was played out under the lamp of public opinion. Everyone—Bob Carpenter, Frank Wiechec, Eddie Sawyer, teammates, sportswriters, baseball fans all over the country—they all watched and measured his progress. But Steinhagen's world after the shooting was much more private. Her relatively short stay in the insane asylum, of course, was confidential, and when she was released, she was able to exist in the shadows of society for decades, quietly living in guarded privacy, at first with her parents, and later in life with her sister, Rita. Ruth Ann Steinhagen—like Eddie Waitkus—would be affected by the night of June 14, 1949, for the rest of her life.

11

All the Game's Wild Glory

In the spring of 1950, Grantland Rice wrote a column dedicated to athletic comebacks and praised Waitkus for his heroic return to the Phillies:

> I'm going back again—
> Perhaps to find the wraith of something lost.
> To miss the contest, and the strife of men,
> And all the game's wild glory, with its cost.
> To certain vanished mornings, slashed with gold,
> To shadows blown at deep dusk from the hills,
> I'm going back again before I'm old,
> Beyond the field of fortune and its thrills.
>
> I'm going back some day.
> Through ghosts and shadows of a losing fight,
> Or cheering crowds that might hold one at bay,
> To find, beyond it all, the peaceful night
> Of quiet valleys, or some friendly lane,
> Where one can hear forgotten songs resung,
> As far, white roads re-echo the refrain
> Of April mornings when the world was young.

"At the end of 54 games last summer," Rice wrote, "Waitkus was hitting .306, when a bullet came within a breath or two of ending his life. And here he's back in a mental and psychological upheaval as well as physical rejuvenation. . . . He gave three years to the war. So he is no kid. But he has been outhustling the kids all spring. The wound in his back, from which spot the bullet was removed is six inches long and at least one inch deep.

In place of waiting until spring to try again, Waitkus went to Florida three months ahead of schedule. He had to win a terrific battle to reach starring condition. Now there is a good chance that 1950 will be the best year he has ever known."

The small clubhouse porch at Clearwater's Athletic Field was soaked in late afternoon sun when the players finished their practice. Some grabbed a cold soda and sat on long wooden benches for a rest; others rushed inside for a shower before heading off to the Beachcomber, a favorite hangout of the Phillies. That was Waitkus's plan. "Hey, Eddie, you got a minute?" asked John Webster, a sports columnist for the *Philadelphia Inquirer.* Waitkus nodded, picked up a couple of icy colas, and the two men settled in at an empty bench at the end of the porch for nearly an hour.

It was mid-March, 1950, and Waitkus was only weeks away from the start of his comeback season. The thirty-year-old Waitkus, sun-tanned and fit, was the center of attention during spring training. He looked healthy, sportswriters agreed, but was he strong enough to play a whole season? And there were rumors he feared the public might considered him a sideshow attraction because of the shooting.

"I was out so long I guess it was just a natural uneasiness about getting back," Waitkus told Webster. "I don't think anything about it now. No, there won't be any unusual pressure this year. This will be a happy season, at that. After all, for a good while I didn't know if I'd stay alive, let alone play ball."

The next day, Webster wrote: "If sun-kissed Edward continues to display the breath-taking stuff he's been flashing these afternoons, he's going to be a tremendous help to those battling Phillies kids this summer. He actually looks better than ever."

Waitkus worked diligently on his own public relations that spring. For nearly four months, he struggled to strengthen his body, faithfully following Wiechec's grueling routine. His only social activity was evening beers with Meyer and Nicholson. But he knew now that spring training was in full swing; now that the other players, the press, and the fans had arrived, he needed to interact with everyone. He wasn't sure if he was emotionally ready. "I don't know if I can trust people the way I used to," he confided to Meyer.

What about women, reporters wanted to know. And what if he got another note from a girl wanting to meet him? "I haven't turned anti-social," Waitkus said, "but I'm afraid I'll leave her a note, telling her to meet me at

Marshall Field's or Wanamakers' window at high noon. And then I'll have her frisked before she comes in. Air-conditioning is okay, but it should never be done with lead in the cool of the evening."

Waitkus was part of a team of young ballplayers who had become known as the Whiz Kids. A carefree group of free-swinging youngsters—the average age of the starting lineup was twenty-six—they began their pennant chase against all odds. Historically, the Phillies languished in the shadow of Connie Mack's popular Philadelphia Athletics, winners of eight American League flags and five world championships. The franchise hadn't won a pennant since 1915. No pitcher on the staff had ever won twenty games in a season, and their starting first baseman had missed more than half the previous season nursing a gunshot wound. But these were the Whiz Kids. They sang in the showers after victories, their top relief pitcher regularly consulted a mortician for pitching advice, and they called each other "Monk," "Houdini," "Puddin' Head," "Bubba," "Swish," "Granny," "Big Cat," and "Slug."

Waitkus was one of the oldest players, but he embodied the Whiz Kids' spirit: "I don't like a guy who beats me at anything. When I play a game, I play to win. That's the way our guys on the Phillies are. They sing and have a beer and horseplay when we win, and they hate the other guy when they lose. That's the way big league baseball should be played, whether you're up top for a pennant or just playing out the season."

Giddy optimism surrounded the Whiz Kids as they completed the exhibition season in early April. On their way north to chilly Philadelphia, the Phillies reeled off five victories in a row, scoring sixty-four runs. The National League president, Ford Frick, was impressed. "The Phillies can win this pennant," he told Grantland Rice, whose syndicated newspaper column alerted the baseball world. "They have youth and speed and a fair amount of power. If their pitching holds up, they can match the Dodgers. Bob Carpenter has gathered a good ball club in a hurry. It wouldn't surprise me to see the Phillies neck and neck with the leaders down the stretch."

In early April, Bob Carpenter, the young owner who hoped 1950 would be the fruition of his years of rebuilding the Phillies, said, "Eddie Waitkus is as fit as any player about to start pennant racing." Waitkus felt a strong loyalty to Carpenter. "The organization has been wonderful to me," he said.

"Of course, it is good business to protect an investment but Bob Carpenter and Eddie Sawyer really have gone beyond what a ballplayer could expect in a game where an injured player all to often is just plumb out of luck. The generous policy of the Phillies is the reason there isn't a player on the club who wouldn't go out and break a leg trying to win."

With a healthy Waitkus at first base, manager Eddie Sawyer made some changes. First, he sent Dick Sisler to left field. Sisler spent four weeks in spring training chasing down fungoes in the outfield, and Frank Wiechec worked tirelessly with Sisler to improve his footwork and speed. With Sisler in left, Del Ennis moved to right, and Richie Ashburn fought off the competition of young prospect Eddie Sanicki and Dick Whitman to keep his starting spot in center. Odd man out in the outfield reshuffle was Waitkus's buddy, veteran Bill Nicholson, who started the season on the Disabled List because of a strained Achilles tendon.

Sawyer was relying on his outfielders to supply most of the Phillies' power. Ennis was a local Philadelphia boy who'd signed with the Phillies right out of high school. In 1949, he hit .302, drove across 110 runs, and had twenty-five home runs. In center, the twenty-three-year-old baby-faced Ashburn had brilliant speed and was considered the team's best bunter. He hit .333 in 1948, led the league with thirty-two stolen bases, and was named Rookie of the Year. Although Sisler lost the first base job to Waitkus, it was his ability to hit the long ball that kept him in the outfield on a daily basis. He'd be tested in the outfield, but Sisler worked hard in the spring, and Sawyer was impressed; Sawyer also liked Sisler's .411 pre-season batting average.

The Phillies' defense was anchored by a smooth infield and solid catching. With Puddin' Head Jones at third, Granny Hamner at short, Mike Goliat at second, Waitkus at first, and Andy Seminick and Stan Lopata sharing the catching duties, the Whiz Kids, most baseball observers agreed, had the best infield and catching in the league. Each infielder, however, threw the ball differently to first base, so Waitkus had to adjust to each style. Jones had a strong overhand motion and frequently pulled Waitkus off the bag with throws that sailed. Hamner was gifted with the strongest arm at his position in the National League, but his sinking throws were the hardest to handle. And Goliat's sidearm motion created some very unpredictable tosses from second base. "I don't know what we'd do without Eddie at first base," said Hamner.

Pitching, however, was a concern for Eddie Sawyer at the start of the season. Only relievers Jim Konstanty and Blix Donnelly and rookie Bob Miller had a spring earned run average under 4.00. Sawyer decided to carry thirteen pitchers to begin the year. Robin Roberts and Curt Simmons headed the starting rotation. Roberts was a hard-throwing right-hander who had signed with the Phillies right out of Michigan State University for $25,000 in 1948. The Phils' prized bonus baby was Simmons, an eighteen-year-old lefty who received $65,000 in 1947. Russ Meyer and thirty-five-year-old Ken Heintzelman, who won seventeen games for the Phillies in 1949, each had a terrible spring, but Sawyer counted on them to round out his four-man rotation. Miller and Bubba Church, also a rookie, would get spot starts, while thirty-three-year-old Konstanty led the bullpen.

Despite Ford Frick's optimism, the Brooklyn Dodgers, defending National League champions, were the overwhelming choice to repeat, according to most scribes. A baseball writers' poll in the *Sporting News* selected Brooklyn to finish first, ahead of the St. Louis Cardinals and the Boston Braves. The Phillies were picked to end the season in fourth, in front of the New York Giants, Pittsburgh Pirates, Cincinnati Reds, and Chicago Cubs.

Waitkus appeared ready for regular-season play, but he knew he had to clear his mind of the memories of the past ten months: Steinhagen's cold eyes when she fired her pawn shop rifle; the surgeries and his painful struggles to survive; fears of never playing ball again; long, doubt-filled nights alone while he recuperated. Doctors assured Waitkus that physically he was okay; everything else, though, was up to him. "The Doc couldn't get up to the plate and hit for me," Waitkus explained. "He couldn't sock Warren Spahn's fastball, Howie Pollet's change of pace, or Dutch Leonard's knuckler. He couldn't go down in the dirt and dig up a low throw from Gran Hamner, or turn a swift grounder into a double play."

Tuesday, April 18, was a cloudy but mild day in Philadelphia, a perfect spring afternoon for opening day. The Swampoodle neighborhood, on the city's North Side, was bursting with excitement. "Lines of traffic from every direction were jammed and tangled. The holiday spirit increased in intensity the closer one came to Shibe Park," the *Evening Bulletin* reported. Shibe Park had opened in 1909 and would be renamed Connie Mack Stadium in 1953. The Phillies began playing there in 1938, when they moved from nearby Baker Bowl. They would share Shibe Park with the Athletics until after the 1954 season, when the A's moved to Kansas City.

Now, long streams of fans stretched in all directions from the corner of Lehigh and 21st Street, the main entrance to Shibe Park. With its beaux arts style of architecture and elaborate three-story domed tower entry, Shibe Park was considered a baseball palace in its time. This opening day, men wore fedoras and coats and ties; servicemen came to the game in uniform; women donned long, wool dress coats and a variety of haberdashery; and school-age children carried their spring jackets, as the slow-moving assemblage made its way toward the park.

Inside, red-white-and-blue bunting decorated the front of the field boxes, and Elliott Lawrence's orchestra played "The Fightin' Phils" just prior to game time. A near-capacity crowd 29,074 fans gave Robin Roberts a raucous ovation when he led the Whiz Kids onto the field. The defending National League champion Brooklyn Dodgers with Jackie Robinson, Gil Hodges, Pee Wee Reese, Duke Snider, Don Newcombe, and Roy Campanella were poised to ruin the Phillies' festive mood, but the Whiz Kids went on to trounce Brooklyn 9–1. Waitkus, although a bit nervous for his return, was strong for the opener. Batting in the third spot, the Shibe Park fans gave him a standing ovation when he walked to the plate for his first at bat. He responded by hitting safely three times and driving home a run. Waitkus had worried that his timing at the plate would be off, but his swing was as smooth as ever. "I was scared to death," he said after the game. "One or two [hits] were lucky ones, but I'd rather be lucky than good."

Good things were happening for Waitkus and the Whiz Kids as the team prepared for their first western trip of the 1950 season. In a game against the Braves at Shibe Park, Waitkus collected four straight hits. By the end of April, he was batting .340 and was a big part of the Whiz Kids' offense. In fifty trips to the plate, he had seventeen hits, four RBIs, six walks and twelve runs scored. Waitkus wasn't the only player off to a good start. Sisler was adjusting well in left field and was hitting the ball with authority, and Roberts's pitching seemed unbeatable. His record went to 3–0 when the Phillies beat Boston 9–3 in the nightcap of a cold and rainy doubleheader in Philadelphia. The Phils ended April winning four out of five against Brooklyn and Boston, winners of the two previous National League flags.

"The Badlands of Chicago," as Waitkus called it, was the initial stop on the Whiz Kids' first trip west. "I just hope I get through this series alive," Waitkus told Nicholson. Waitkus and the Phillies spent two nights at the Edgewater Beach, and Waitkus was a bit jittery about returning to the lake-front hotel. He told Nicholson, "This time, Nick, don't leave me out of your sight." The Edgewater Beach, according to Meyer, posted an armed security guard at the front desk when the Phillies arrived. "See that guy, Eddie, he's there just because of you," Meyer told Waitkus. The three former Cubs—Waitkus, Nicholson, and Meyer—revisited their usual favorite Chicago nightspots, including the bar at the Sheridan Plaza, and spent their two nights at the Edgewater without any incidents.

Waitkus went one-for-four and played perfectly at first base in his return to Wrigley Field, but the Phillies lost to the Cubs 10–8. The Whiz Kids rebounded to win the next afternoon, and they went on to win two out of three from the Cardinals, to win three straight against the Reds, and to beat the Pirates in the final game of the road trip. "Our clubhouse was becoming pretty loose—everyone was having a great time," Meyer said years later. "The guys sang in the shower after each win, especially Waitkus and Sisler. I think we all knew we were going places."

On the afternoon of May 12, the Capitol Limited pulled into Philadelphia's B and 0 Railroad station. Hitched to the rear of the train were four special cars carrying the Phillies and the Boston Braves, who were making their way home from Chicago. Several hundred cheering fans greeted the Whiz Kids' arrival. The crowd exploded with huge cheers for Sisler, Waitkus, and Meyer, and someone yelled at Sawyer, "Keep 'em going, Eddie, let's have a pennant." The Braves, huddled against the windows of their Pullmans, watched with envy.

The weather during first month of the season was miserable, with cold temperatures all around the league, but Waitkus swung a hot bat. He hit .321 and played flawlessly at first base. Waitkus gained more and more confidence at the plate with each at bat. His swing was smooth and graceful, and his coordination was sharp. By the middle of May, he had slashed thirty-five hits, including one home run, one triple, and four doubles. His hitting style was the same as before the shooting. Never trying to overswing, he took outside pitches to left field, and when a pitcher came inside, he pulled in his hands and drilled the ball to right. Physically, he was strong, and emotionally, he appeared relaxed and confident.

But by June, the stress of playing virtually every day soon affected him; Waitkus struggled throughout the month; in 105 at bats, he hit an anemic .200. He began to get fatigued in the later innings and went to trainer Frank Wiechec regularly for "pep-up" injections of vitamin C; Wiechec and other athletic trainers believed ascorbic acid gave the players more stamina. Waitkus also went to Wiechec for amphetamines—such as Benzedrine or Dexedrine—to stimulate his run-down body.

Waitkus may have been struggling, but heading into the All Star game, the Phillies went on a roll. They won nine of twelve and led the league by a full game. The early-July All Star break came at a perfect time for Waitkus. In desperate need of rest, he returned to his home near Boston and watched the game on television. A year ago, as an honorary member of the National League team, Waitkus listened to the game from his hospital bed, wondering if he'd ever be healthy enough to play again. Now, midway through the baseball season, Waitkus was having doubts again. All through June, he had been unable to sustain his stamina and strength, and he worried that he'd be too weak to perform at a high level during the intensity of a pennant race. The adhesions in his back muscles made it difficult at times to stretch for throws at first base. And despite the fact he'd suffered from a collapsed lung following the shooting, he had started smoking cigarettes again, which further hurt his stamina. He was also drinking, believing that if he worked out daily the alcohol wouldn't bother him. But, in fact, alcohol became a problem for Waitkus, one that would plague him for the rest of his life. He put in long hours at the bar of Philadelphia's fashionable Warwick Hotel. As his play on the field worsened and as he became more anxious about his strength, his visits to the Warwick increased. There, after Shibe Park home games, he'd commiserate with bartender and friend Danny Lanni; it was a routine, some teammates said, as addictive as the alcohol. According to many of his close friends, the more he worried—about his playing ability, his health, and his total recovery—the more he drank.

Waitkus also used the All Star break to continue his relationship with Carol Webel, the girl he met at Clearwater Beach. Feeling despondent, Waitkus telephoned Carol, who lived with her parents in Albany, New York. Carol always had a way of relaxing and inspiring Waitkus. They agreed to meet in Philadelphia and New York for dinner whenever their schedules would allow it, and they made plans to visit each other's families once the season was over. They made the best of their long-distance romance; whenever Carol had a chance to get to Philadelphia, they frequented the city's after-hours clubs, took in the latest Bogart movie, or spent quiet time listening to Tony Martin or Frank Sinatra.

After the All Star game, as the Phillies and the Cardinals battled daily for control of first place, Sawyer decided to make some changes in his batting order. Waitkus was getting on base, but he wasn't hitting with power, so Sawyer moved him to the leadoff spot. Ashburn, a great bunter, was dropped to the second slot, and Sisler replaced Waitkus as the team's third hitter.

The move worked well right from the start. Waitkus went five-for-five against the Reds in Cincinnati in the nightcap of a twin bill. In the sixth inning, he doubled for his fourth straight hit off Ewell Blackwell. When Waitkus pulled up at second base, Blackwell stared at him and said, "You'd better be loose up there next time, for you're going down." Blackwell never got a chance to deck Waitkus. Johnny Hetki replaced him on the mound but had no better luck against Waitkus, who singled to cap his perfect day at the plate.

In the final days of June, the North Korean People's Army had crossed the thirty-eighth parallel and invaded the Republic of South Korea. President Harry Truman had quickly sent U.S. air and naval support to the South Koreans and ordered American foot soldiers to South Korea. The Korean War would have a profound effect on the Whiz Kids. On August 1, Curt Simmons, a member of the Pennsylvania National Guard, was drafted. Simmons, at age twenty-one, became the first major leaguer called for active duty in Korea. When his unit was activated in early September, Simmons had a 17–8 record. Bob Carpenter now worried that an escalation in the draft would obliterate his young club. The loss of Simmons during the stretch drive was a tremendous blow. Roberts and Simmons were the best one-two pitching combination in the league. Sawyer usually pitched them back-to-back, and when one didn't win, the other did. Most of the time, though, they scored consecutive victories.

The Phillies were also hurting physically during the stretch drive. Ted Kluszewski, a muscle-bound power hitter with the Reds, smashed a line drive off the face of Bubba Church, who had to be carried off the field. The next day, Bob Miller pulled a muscle in his shoulder. Dick Sisler played with a sprained wrist, Del Ennis had a severe charley horse in his leg, and Andy

Seminick struggled through the final week with a broken bone in his left ankle. And in early September, Nicholson, who'd dropped fourteen pounds in a two-week period because of diabetes, was lost to the team for the rest of the year. The season was also taking its toll on Waitkus. He began losing weight in the hot August sun, and by early September, he had lost nearly ten pounds. "The bat seems to be getting awful heavy," he admitted. Waitkus, though, was hitting the ball well, and the leadoff spot was a perfect fit for him. He maintained a .285 average, but strength and stamina was the problem.

"What an ordeal the last six weeks were," he told his friend, sportswriter Frank Yeutter. "I'd get up in the morning just as tired and jittery as when I went to bed. I roomed with Bill Nicholson, and I knew he was a sick man. He kept losing weight all the time. Between worrying about the team and not being able to get to sleep myself, then seeing Nick get worse, I was in a horrible mental state.

"I've often wondered how many different kinds of 'pep' pills Frank Wiechec bought. All of us were taking energy-building medicines. Every time Frank found a new pill in his medical book he bought a load of them. I took eight different kinds of pills in one day, and I was just as dead on my feet as if I'd taken none of them."

The atmosphere in the locker room of pennant contenders in the final weeks of the stretch drive can be tense, especially when the conversation turns to money and the World Series. Waitkus, tired and aching from the daily strain of a tight pennant race, was dressing after a Shibe Park night game when a young reporter, searching for a fresh story, stopped at his locker.

"That five grand World Series money won't be hard to take about the middle of October will it, Eddie?"

"Nope," Waitkus said, looking into a small mirror that was hung on the inside of his locker door. Waitkus was much more interested in fashioning a perfect Windsor knot in his new silk tie than answering the question. But he continued: "It will come in right handy even if Uncle Sam does get a big part of it. But that isn't all that goes with winning a pennant. It's the thrill of playing in the World Series."

"Yeh, but that big dough has a lot to do with it." The writer knew that if he kept at it, Waitkus would hand him his story.

"I disagree." Waitkus turned and looked the youngster straight in the face. "Do you think a good ballplayer goes out there every day thinking of only what's in it for him? If he did he'd be a second division player. You can't beat nine other guys thinking of your bank balance. It takes base hits. It takes pitching and it takes nine guys playing as a team."

"There may be some old pros who think that way," the reporter shot back, "but when a race is as close as this one, and four clubs have a chance for it, there's got to be a thought of the money involved."

"You talk about old pros. Do you think Joe DiMaggio got out there last year and almost single-handedly batted the Red Sox out of a pennant just for a few bucks? He's a rich man. He was hurting all over. He didn't even know if he could even swing a bat. Money players would have gone on the voluntary retired list. But not DiMaggio. He went in and played like a champion." Waitkus had made his point, but he wasn't finished. "And another thing, I don't like those guys who use a game just to become national figures. Take those tennis players who lose a big match and then jump across the net and shake hands and say 'well-played old fellow.' That's the bunk."

Waitkus went back to his Windsor as the reporter scribbled in his notebook.

The 1950 season finally came down to a pair of games at Brooklyn. The Dodgers could force a playoff if they swept the Phils, and that's exactly the way it appeared after the Dodgers won the first game 7–3. When the Phillies entered their Ebbets Field locker room after the game, they found a radio broadcast remote setup in one corner of the room. The radio technicians had been traveling with the Phillies during the past several days, waiting to bring the victory celebration back to the listening audience in Philadelphia. "Get that thing out of here," yelled coach Benny Bengough. "We've had it around for the whole week and it's brought nothing but a lot of bad luck."

Sunday, October 1, was bright and sunny in Flatbush. Cozy Ebbets Field overflowed with 35,073 baseball fanatics, and Brooklyn police turned away another 25,000. The Phillies and Dodgers, each with 153 games behind them, were back where they had started on opening day: Roberts versus Newcombe. "It's all up to you," Sawyer told his young ace, who was making his third start in five days. Brooklyn's Burt Shotton, who managed his team in a Dodgers-blue warm-up jacket and a blue bow tie with white polka dots, had all the confidence in the world in Newcombe. Each pitcher had nineteen victories; it was Roberts's sixth try for number twenty.

Roberts and Newcombe were pitching brilliantly. The game was tied 1–1 in the bottom of the ninth when Cal Abrams reached first base on a walk. Reese followed with a hit, moving Abrams to second. Many observers thought it was a perfect sacrifice situation, but Shotton decided against it. Duke Snider made his manager look like a genius when he lashed a sharp base hit to center. But the Dodgers' third base coach, Milt Stock, who'd played third base on the Phillies' 1915 pennant-winning team, made a horrible decision. With none out, he waved home Abrams. Ashburn charged Snider's hit and fired a one-hop strike to Lopata, who received the ball a few feet up the baseline. Abrams had no chance and was out by several feet. "A routine play," Ashburn said later.

Reese and Snider took second and third on the throw home, and the Phillies walked Jackie Robinson intentionally to load the bases. Roberts was still in trouble. With only one out, almost any type of fly ball to the outfield would easily score the speedy Reese from third. With the Brooklyn fans howling on every pitch, the next batter, Carl Furillo, popped out to Waitkus, and Gil Hodges flew out to Ennis in right. Reese, Snider, Robinson, Furillo, and Hodges, Roger Kahn's fabled "Boys of Summer," went at the Whiz Kids with everything and came up short.

Sawyer let Roberts hit for himself as the Phillies opened the tenth inning. He had a couple of potential pinch hitters in Dick Whitman and Jack Mayo on the bench, but Sawyer wanted his ace to pitch the bottom of the tenth. Roberts responded by hitting the second pitch to center for a base hit. Waitkus followed, and the Dodgers' infield moved in, expecting a bunt. Waitkus took the first pitch for a called strike and then tried to bunt, but the ball went foul. Ahead in the count, Newcombe made a crucial two-strike mistake, and Waitkus punched a Texas leaguer to center for a hit. Ashburn, the team's premier bunter, laid down a what appeared to be a perfect sacrifice, but Newcombe sprung from the mound and threw out Roberts at third. Dick Sisler, his sprained wrist wrapped in tape, walked to the plate, the fourth straight left-handed batter to face Newcombe.

Eddie Waitkus stood on second base, poised to live out every ballplayer's dream. Standing in the middle of the field, at the epicenter of one of baseball's great games, Waitkus remained remarkably placid. On this cool October afternoon, fifteen and a half months after a crazed teenage girl had nearly ended his life, Waitkus was about to complete his successful comeback. His back ached and he was exhausted, but this was the moment he had struggled for. Sisler, who had tagged Newcombe for three straight hits, looked beyond the big pitcher and saw Waitkus take a cautious leadoff. The two men who fought so hard in March for the same job were about to win a pennant for the Phillies. Sisler refocused on Newcombe as Waitkus inched toward third.

Sitting in a box seat behind the Dodgers dugout, George Sisler, then the head scout for Brooklyn, watched his son reach out and hit Newcombe's fifth pitch toward the left field bleachers. Abrams, his body limp against the shoe polish advertisement on the outfield wall, watched the baseball soar into the crowd. The Phillies erupted. The entire team jumped out of the dugout, stormed past home plate umpire Larry Goetz, and mobbed Sisler. The Whiz Kids, with a 4–1 lead, were three outs away from a championship.

Roberts's gutsy pitching, Ashburn's perfect throw, Waitkus's two-strike hit, and Sisler's dramatic home run stunned the Dodgers. They went out meekly in their final at bats, three up, three down. The Phillies rushed the mound and carried Roberts off the field. Everybody but Frank Wiechec. The Phillies' trainer jumped out of the dugout and sprinted toward Waitkus, and the two men hugged and jumped on the diamond like little leaguers.

A thin and pale Eddie Waitkus was physically and emotionally drained as the Phillies prepared to host the World Series. His weight loss during the summer—nearly twenty pounds—had become very noticeable, even to the fans. Waitkus's white flannel uniform hung on his slender frame, and the number 4 on his jersey seemed to cover his entire back. When the chilly autumn breeze whipped across the infield, his red pinstripes ballooned like a full-blown spinnaker at first base. Just one year ago, Waitkus was fighting for his baseball life. Now he was hanging on again, trying to gather enough stamina and strength for one more series, the most important in his career. "Skip, the bat feels like a telephone pole in my hands, and I've never been so whipped, but I'll come through, I promise," he told his manager. But Waitkus didn't tell Sawyer that he planned to see a doctor as soon as the Series ended.

For 101 of the 167 days of the 1950 season, the Phillies occupied first place, moving in and out of the top spot seven times. They won ninety-one games and lost sixty-three. Eddie Waitkus surprised everyone, including himself, by playing in 154 games. "I thought I'd be lucky to play in 75 games," he said. Waitkus hit .284 and led the National League with 143 singles. He also set personal career highs in three categories: 102 runs scored, 182 hits, and thirty-two doubles. Ennis's 126 RBIs was tops in the league, and Ashburn led everyone with fourteen triples. As a team, the Phillies hit .265.

Shibe Park and the surrounding neighborhood blossomed in red-white-and-blue bunting for the opening of the World Series. Sixteen colorful pennants—one for every team in the majors—lined the park, and streets, storefronts, and homes flew the "Fightin' Phils" colors of red and white. Ticket "agencies" sprang up overnight; scalpers were getting $70 for an $8.75 box seat. Caught up in the excitement, Bob Carpenter even ordered new infield sod for the Series.

Topcoat weather greeted the Phils and Yanks for game one. Although he was taken off the eligible list, Private First Class Curt Simmons, on a ten-day furlough from the army, was in a Phillies uniform pitching batting practice. And Bill Nicholson, who spent most of September in a hospital to get his diabetes under control, was back with his teammates offering morale support. "Eddie wasn't in much better shape that I was," Nicholson said. "He should have been in the hospital with me because he was so weak and tired during August and September. I don't know how he made it through the stretch drive, and he played such a good World Series too."

Waitkus hit a respectable .267 in the Series, although the Phillies fell to the Yankees in four straight games. He collected four hits in fifteen official at bats, walked twice, and executed a perfectly placed sacrifice bunt; and the powerful Yankee pitchers failed to strike him out. Waitkus made no errors at first base, recording thirty-four putouts and three assists. As a team, the Phillies hit just .203; the free-swinging Whiz Kids chased high fastball after high fastball with no success. New York manager Casey Stengel said that this had been his strategy: "A free-swinging club like Philadelphia is usually a lowball hitting team, but can't hit the high ones too well. We had our pitchers throw high and keep going higher if they chased the high pitches."

Unlike most of his teammates, Waitkus was anything but a free-swinging hitter. He was a patient, contact hitter, a disciplined leadoff man, especially against a hard-throwing pitching staff. Because he was so tired and weak, Waitkus made a determined effort to stay back, to wait at the plate for pitches, rather than swinging wildly at balls outside the strike zone. The strategy worked; Waitkus reached base safely six times, but he failed to score because the Phillies' big hitters fell into Stengel's trap and swung under, over, and through high fastballs in all four games.

Manager Eddie Sawyer surprised most everyone by giving Jim Kostanty the ball in game one. It was Konstanty's first starting assignment ever as a Phillie. Sawyer knew Robin Roberts, who had pitched three games in the final five days of the season, needed more rest, and Bubba Church and Bob Miller were not fully recovered from their late-season injuries. Stengel went to his ace, Vic Raschi.

In his first World Series at bat, Waitkus, the Phils' leadoff hitter, slapped a pitch down the left-field line. Gene Woodling gave chase, but the ball sliced into the lower boxes, and Woodling fell to his knees and crashed into the short wall, near the Phillies' bullpen. Waitkus eventually ended his first World Series plate appearance by fouling out to catcher Yogi Berra. Waitkus drew a walk in the sixth inning, but he went oh-for-three in the game. In the Yankee fourth, Bobby Brown, batting left-handed, reached out and hit a pitch off the end of his bat down the left-field line. The ball skipped over third base and caromed off the wall protecting the left-field boxes. By the time Sisler retrieved the baseball, Brown was standing on second base. Hank Bauer hit a towering fly ball that chased Ashburn to the deepest part of center field. Richie made a great grab 425 feet from the plate, but Brown had no trouble advancing to third after the catch. Jerry Coleman then flew out to Sisler, scoring Brown. That lone run was all Raschi needed; the Yanks won the opener 1–0.

Waitkus's first World Series hit came in the third inning of game two when he pulled an Allie Reynolds fastball down the right-field line for a double, but he was left stranded when Ashburn fouled out and Sisler was thrown out by second baseman Jerry Coleman to end the inning. With the score tied 1–1 in the fifth, Goliat opened the inning with a single to left, and after Roberts, who attempted to sacrifice, popped out to the pitcher, Waitkus singled to right. He hit a ground ball directly to Coleman, but the ball hit a stone and bounced over the fielder's head; Goliat advanced to third on the play and scored on Ashburn's sacrifice fly. The scored remained tied until Joe DiMaggio stepped to the plate to lead off the tenth. DiMaggio had popped out four straight times against Roberts's rising fastball and hadn't hit the ball out of the infield in the two World Series games. Behind in the count, Roberts threw a low, inside fastball on two-and-one. DiMaggio dipped down and golfed the baseball deep into the left-field bleachers to give the Yankees a 2–1 lead.

The Whiz Kids battled back in the bottom of the tenth. Jack Mayo, hitting for Roberts, walked. Waitkus then dropped down a perfect sacrifice bunt toward third, advancing Mayo to second. But Ashburn and Sisler were quickly retired, and Mayo, along with the Phillies' hopes for a home victory, died at second base. The Yankees left Philadelphia with a 2–1 victory and a 2–0 Series lead.

When the Series moved to Yankee Stadium, Ken Heintzelman, who had won only three games during the season, took the mound for the Whiz Kids against Ed Lopat. Waitkus, who years later told his son that one of his biggest baseball thrills was playing in Yankee Stadium, opened the game with a single to right. But Ashburn, after failing to sacrifice Waitkus, struck out. Waitkus moved to second on an infield out, but he was left there when Ennis bounced out to end the inning. Heintzelman took a 2–1 lead into the eighth inning, but after quickly retiring Woodling and Rizzuto, he suddenly lost everything. Jerry Coleman coaxed a walk, and Berra and DiMaggio walked on eight straight pitches to load the bases. Sawyer had seen enough of Heintzelman and brought in Konstanty. Brown pinch-hit for Hank Bauer and rolled a routine ground ball to short, but Hamner booted the ball, allowing Coleman to score the tying run. The Yankees pushed across a run in the ninth to win 3–2 and were now one victory away from a sweep.

On October 7, Waitkus played in his final World Series game. Despite his weakened condition, he was still able to hold his concentration at the plate and in the field. After working Whitey Ford to a full count in the first inning, Waitkus walked. For the second game in a row, Waitkus led off the game by getting on base. Ashburn flied out to Woodling, but Puddin' Head Jones hit a ground-rule double to right, advancing Waitkus to third. Ennis then chopped a bouncer to Brown at third base. Waitkus ran hard on the contact play, but Brown charged the ball and threw a strike to Berra to barely get Waitkus at the plate. Sisler ended the inning by looking at strike three.

In the third inning, Waitkus collected his fourth World Series hit when he singled to center. Again he failed to score as Ford struck out Ashburn and got Jones to hit into a fielder's choice. The Yankees eventually won the game 5–2 to complete the sweep. In the Phillies' locker room, Waitkus's calm reaction following the defeat reflected his persona: honest but always choosing carefully measured words, always very reflective. Waitkus said, "I think there was a letdown, especially after that last game [of the regular season]. Perhaps if we had won [the pennant] four or five days before, then we could have gotten mentally prepared. We went as far as we did, and I think it was quite an accomplishment."

That evening, the Whiz Kids boarded a train for Philadelphia. They talked quietly in their Pullmans about travel plans. Some would return to their winter homes immediately, others made dates for the opening of deer season. Waitkus told Meyer, "I'm exhausted. I don't know how I made it. I'm going to find a beach, stick my head in the sand, and never come out."

12

Hero's Journey

After the final game of the World Series, Eddie Waitkus stepped on the scales in the visitors' clubhouse at Yankee Stadium. He weighed less than 160 pounds. "I hadn't weighed that little since high school," he told a teammate.

The long baseball season of 1950 and the stress of the pennant stretch drive hit Waitkus hard. Physically and mentally, he was exhausted. Days after the World Series, he entered Boston's Leahy Clinic for an series of medical tests. He was anemic, his nerves were on edge, and he was having trouble sleeping. "There were so many things wrong with me I thought I needed a mortician," Waitkus said. "I was certainly coffin bait."

His doctors ordered rest, plenty of it, so Waitkus headed for Florida in November. Clearwater Beach became his sanctuary, a place where he could always relax, become stronger, and get his thoughts together. This is where he had overcome his physical and psychological fears following the shooting and where he made himself into a baseball player again. Waitkus spent several weeks resting on Clearwater Beach, and again he became rejuvenated in the Florida sun. He gained fifteen pounds and spent his days as a self-confessed beachcomber.

Veteran Philadelphia baseball writer Frank Yeutter was a close friend of Waitkus. Yeutter, like Waitkus, was a history buff, and he found Eddie's intellect refreshing. Yeutter described Waitkus as "a debonair, sharp tongued, urbane New Englander, always ready with a quip, always humming the latest tune." Yeutter and Waitkus enjoyed each other's company, and their conversations usually transcended baseball. And they occasionally drank together. When Yeutter covered the baseball winter meetings in St. Petersburg, he took the opportunity to find his old friend.

"The sun splashed against the side of an unpainted building at Clearwater Beach," wrote Yeutter. "Lazily propped against the wall sat a plump, drowsing character. As I drove up and stepped out, the sunbather took a disinterested look then went back to his catnap. But only for one second. He jerked his head up; his eyes opened, blinked a couple of times, and then came a surprised yelp. 'Oh. No, don't tell me.'

"That was the greeting Eddie Waitkus had at our first meeting since the 1950 World Series. But what a different Waitkus! During those last few weeks of the season when the Phillies came within a whisker of losing their first pennant in 35 years, Eddie was tired, drawn and exhausted. Waitkus is positively corpulent. He's burned the color of a deep-sea fisherman. He still adheres to the crew haircut, but the sun has bleached his hair until it is taffy colored."

The two friends spent the next few hours catching up at the Beachcomber, a favorite watering hole of the Phillies players, coaches, and reporters, not far from Waitkus's yacht basin apartment. Yeutter had a notepad full of questions on a variety of subjects, including marriage rumors.

"First of all, let's get this marital thing straightened out," said Waitkus. "I'm not engaged. That whole story started when my girl and her parents came to New York to see us play. She's a swell girl, too."

The reporter wanted more.

"Sure, I'll tell you her name. It's Carol Webel and she lives in Albany, New York. She's the one and only. That's true. But we're not engaged yet."

Although he didn't elaborate with Yeutter, Waitkus was very much in love. As they had planned during the 1950 All Star break, Carol visited Waitkus's family in Melrose once the World Series was over. She spent time getting to know Waitkus's father, Stephen, and his sister, Stella. And one week later, in late October, amid newspaper reports he and Carol were planning a wedding, Waitkus traveled to Albany for Carol's birthday. Syndicated columnist Walter Winchell wrote that Waitkus and Carol were about to be married. Waitkus gave Carol a diamond studded wrist watch for her birthday but no engagement ring. He told the local press, "I just came over to deliver Carol's birthday present in person and spend the weekend with her. Carol and I are just good friends, and any talk about wedding plans is pretty premature. You know how it is in my business. Any time you date a girl, the papers expect a wedding announcement."

Carol and Waitkus continued their romance during the winter, and as

Winchell prematurely predicted, made quiet plans for a wedding, though not until November 1951. During the 1951 baseball season, they met several times in Philadelphia and New York, and Carol became friendly with some of the Phillies' wives, especially Nancy Nicholson and Mary Meyer. "My father swept my mother off her feet during their courtship," their daughter, Ronni, said years later. "The Florida atmosphere, the baseball players, the fine dinner spots. It was a very romantic courtship."

Carol knew nothing about baseball, and that was just fine with Waitkus. She was attracted to him because of his sensitivity and his intelligence. "Eddie was a sentimentalist about so many things, like poetry and songs, and I like that," she said. "He was so different than most baseball players. Baseball wasn't the only thing in his life. But it was his pursuit of knowledge that I admired so much. Eddie was always sensitive when he discussed what was going on in the world. He had his opinions, but he was always thoughtful and not debatable."

Carol, the young woman he met on Clearwater Beach, had become Waitkus's soul mate during those dark months of rehabilitation following the shooting. She was the girl, he often said, who resurrected his heart and his trust in people. This was someone, he told his pal Russ Meyer, with whom he could spend the rest of his life. "She relaxes me, and, I know this sounds corny, but she inspires me," he said.

Waitkus was physically fit and emotionally refreshed for the new baseball year. He began the season as baseball's Comeback Player of the Year. The Associated Press writers voted Waitkus the honor following his brilliant performance in 1950. "It was only seventeen months ago that Waitkus tottered on the brink of death, critically wounded by a bullet fired by a crazed girl in Chicago," the A.P. reported. "Few thought he would live, much less play baseball again. But this blond of Lithuanian ancestry showed them all, including himself."

Heading into the new season, everyone in the Phillies organization was looking to build on the success of the year before. Management wanted a World Series championship and another Shibe Park attendance record. Players wanted more money. After all, they reasoned, 1,217,080 peopled passed through the turnstiles, an increase of nearly 400,000 from 1949. And fans talked about a Whiz Kids' dynasty. But only the players got what they wanted.

The 1951 baseball season was a disaster for the Phillies and also a disappointment for Waitkus. The Fightin' Phils had no fight in them. They won only seventy-three games and finished in fifth place, twenty-three and a half games behind the league-leading Giants. Shibe Park attendance fell by 279,377, and manager Eddie Sawyer blamed his players. "All that World Series money went to their heads in '51," he said. "They thought they'd win games by just showing up." Waitkus batted just .257, far below his previous career mark of .293, and his statistics were down in every major category: He scored only sixty-five runs, down from 102; collected 157 hits, compared to 182; hit twenty-seven doubles, five fewer than the year before; and his on-base percentage fell from .341 to .317.

Waitkus wasn't sure why he played so poorly; "Maybe it was a normal letdown after all the emotion of 1950," he told Bill Nicholson. But according to his manager, Waitkus failed because he didn't take care of himself during the long season. "Waitkus isn't strong enough to party at night the way he does and be ready for games the next day," Sawyer said. Those comments, although true, ruined his relationship with Waitkus. "It really ended their friendship," Nicholson said, "because Eddie figured Sawyer wanted him off the team. Heck, most of us struggled that year, and quite frankly, most of us partied too much, but Sawyer chose to single out Eddie."

Waitkus was correct—the Phillies were looking to trade him. Bob Carpenter wanted to get a first baseman with power, possibly Earl Torgeson of the Braves, Gil Hodges of the Dodgers, or Ted Kluszewski of the Reds. And Waitkus wasn't the only player on the trading block. Following the 1951 season, Carpenter, upset with the Phillies' fifth-place finish, said every player—except Roberts and Ashburn—was available. Because of his consistent hitting and fine glove, Waitkus remained valuable trade bait for the next two years.

And there was also the Tom Casagrande experiment. Casagrande was a twenty-year-old left-handed pitcher and slugger from Fordham University. He stood six-foot-three and weighed 225 pounds, and he had an even bigger reputation. "Another Babe Ruth," some scouts predicted. Eight major league clubs fought to acquire Casagrande, but a bonus check for $40,000 convinced the youngster to sign with the Phillies. Casagrande was assigned to the Phillies' Terre Haute farm club for the 1951 season, but he worked out with the Phillies at Clearwater Beach during spring training.

Sawyer soon became disenchanted with Casagrande's pitching, but he thought his bat had potential. "Teach the kid how to play first base," Sawyer told Waitkus. One year after Waitkus had worked so hard to win back his job as a major league first baseman, he was ordered to teach some kid right out of college how to play his position. For the next few weeks, Waitkus slowly guided Casagrande through the basics, and in doing so, refined his own skills. "Teaching Tom has taught me things I didn't know myself, has brushed me up on some of the things I was getting careless in," Waitkus said. "It has also taught me how to teach. I have watched his reactions to my words, my actions. It has been like going to school, learning to be a teacher. Working with Tom has sharpened me mentally as well as physically."

One morning in the Phillies' Clearwater dugout, someone asked Casagrande how the lessons were going and whether he thought he'd make it to the majors as a first baseman. "I'll learn how to play the bag with Eddie helping me and then I'll come back to cause a lot of people some worry—but never Eddie," he said. However, Casagrande's confidence—and bat—fell short. The Ruthian power never materialized, so he went back to pitching. He bounced around the Phillies' farm system for a few years but never made it to the majors.

In early September of 1951, as the Phillies' baseball season slowly and painfully wound down, Waitkus formally announced he was engaged to Carol Webel, about one year after Walter Winchell's wedding "scoop." Actually it was Waitkus himself who was responsible for Winchell's report. In September of 1950, as the Phillies were waiting out a rain delay at Braves Field in Boston, Waitkus had told his old friend, baseball writer Frank Wheeler, "You know I think I'll get married in November. I think it's time I settled down. Funny thing, I almost lost my life when that girl shot me last year, yet I found the future Mrs. Waitkus as a result of it. We met while I was down at Clearwater where our trainer, Frank Wiechec, was putting me through conditioning exercises that enabled me to play ball again. The girl's name is Carol Webel and she lives in Albany, New York. She's a laboratory technician and a college graduate." Waitkus's quotation ran in the Boston press and Winchell picked it up for his national column. But Waitkus—and Carol—spent the next year denying they were engaged. Waitkus, apparently caught up in romance, spoke a bit prematurely—about one year prematurely.

On a chilly November Sunday in 1951, Eddie Waitkus and Carol Webel did become man and wife. With Bill Nicholson as best man, they were married in a formal ceremony at Albany's St. Patrick's Roman Catholic Church. Waitkus's boyhood friends from East Cambridge, including Frank Sharka and Leonard Frisoli, and family members from Melrose and Boston, arrived the night before the wedding for a private party at the Ten Eyck Hotel. The wedding was major news in Albany. One local society page headline quipped: "Big Leaguer Takes Albany Bride—Eddie Waitkus Will Play Second Now." More than 150 guests attended—including many of the Whiz Kids—and scores of kids waited outside the church, eager to get a close look at the major leaguers. Following the ceremony, a police escort led the bridal party to the Ten Eyck for a lavish reception. Eddie and Carol honeymooned on Clearwater Beach, agreeing to live in Philadelphia during the baseball season and in Albany in the fall and winter.

Yet life was taking yet another new turn for Waitkus. He seemed at ease in his marriage to Carol, but as an athlete, he again was on the edge. The glory of 1950 remained alive only in the minds of baseball romantics; the disappointing reality of the 1951 season assured that. At season's end, Waitkus knew three things: his 1952 contract would include a hefty pay cut; the Phillies would continue to do everything possible to trade him; and he would never again be friends with Eddie Sawyer.

13

In the Shadows

With the 1952 baseball season just two days old, Ruth Ann Steinhagen, her parents, and her attorney posed for news photographers outside Chicago's Cook County Criminal Court building. Her stay in the state mental hospital over, Steinhagen appeared poised and happy; she presented a polished and tailored look. Conservatively dressed in a full length dress, high-heel pumps, and a long swing-coat, Steinhagen held her parents' arms and smiled. She had survived her confinement, would escape further imprisonment, and was free to begin a new life.

Steinhagen had spent thirty-three months in the Kankakee State Hospital and, according to Dr. Ernest Klein, the hospital's superintendent, had responded "favorably" to electric shock treatment. Shortly before her release, she told the *Chicago Herald American:* "Since the night I lured Waitkus to my room at the Edgewater Beach Hotel in order to shoot him, I have made the world's longest journey. I have come back to sanity from the fog-shrouded world where I groped my way. There never will be any words to tell how grateful I am. I am grateful to Eddie Waitkus, who never showed the least wish to be revenged on me for my crazy attempt to kill him. I no longer have any desire to see him or write to him." But a few days later, after hospital officials declared her sane and discharged her, she said, "I intend to write Waitkus to tell him he has nothing to fear, that the shooting was the act of a sick girl and is now a forgotten chapter in my life. I want his mind to be at ease."

Waitkus said he never received any correspondence from Steinhagen. However, he admitted to his close friend Russ Meyer that he was concerned for his safety for years because of a statement Steinhagen made shortly after her arrest in 1949. She told authorities at Chicago's Cook County jail: "If I ever get out of here I'll kill him for sure if he ever gets married. He's the only one worth shooting. I wouldn't shoot anybody else."

After leaving Kankakee in late March, Steinhagen returned to Cook County jail to await her sanity hearing and to face an outstanding charge of assault with intent to kill. Waitkus heard about Steinhagen's release from the mental hospital while at spring training. "I hope I never have to hear anything more about her or the affair," he said. "It's water over the dam with me." But in early April, he said: "I'd like to find out what's happening there. I'm going to call the district attorney when we get [to Chicago] and ask him about it. I wouldn't want to be responsible for releasing her. How can people go around blowing holes in other people and then be allowed to go free?" A few days later, according to Edward Breen, first assistant state's attorney in Chicago, Waitkus told him he had decided not to prosecute Steinhagen and "wanted to forget the entire incident." Waitkus's wife, Carol, said he did not prosecute because he did not want to become heavily involved in the publicity of a protracted, high-profile, out-of-state, criminal trial; Waitkus also never pursued any civil action against Steinhagen.

On April 17, Steinhagen was adjudged sane and freed of the assault with intent to kill charge; the legal process took just one hour. Dr. William Haines, the first psychiatrist to examine Steinhagen following the shooting, told a jury in the courtroom of Judge Daniel A. Covelli that he agreed with the mental hospital's opinion that Steinhagen had indeed recovered her sanity. Haines, the chief psychiatrist of the Cook County Behavior Clinic, provided the court with this official diagnosis: "Without active mental disease at this time. She knows the nature of the charge and is able to cooperate with her counsel." Haines also told the court he believed she was insane at the time of the shooting. Ten minutes later, the jury found Steinhagen to be sane. This officially freed her from confinement, leaving it up to the discretion of the state's attorney whether to prosecute Steinhagen on the outstanding 1949 charge of assault with intent to kill. An assistant state's attorney then asked Dr. Haines if he would testify that Steinhagen was sane if she were tried on the charge. Haines said he would; the state, knowing Waitkus would not prosecute and that Steinhagen was insane at the time of the shooting, then asked the court to nullify prosecution, clearing the way for Steinhagen's freedom.

On the steps of the Cook County Criminal Court building following her sanity hearing, Steinhagen stood tall between her mother and father. She grinned and calmly posed for photos and said she thought she might return to Kankakee State Hospital to practice occupational therapy, a skill, she said, she learned as a patient. Ruth Ann Steinhagen, now twenty-two years old, kissed her lawyer, walked down the courthouse stairs, and climbed into the back seat of a black sedan. A long shadow swept the sidewalk as the car slowly merged with traffic.

The transition Steinhagen made from the state mental hospital to the outside world was not easy. Kankakee State Hospital was a benevolent society with a small-town, community atmosphere that provided a warm, protective environment for her. Mental patients in the early 1950s were sent home from state facilities with little or no counseling or follow-up, so returning to mainstream society was a huge challenge. When Steinhagen left Kankakee, she returned home to her parents and younger sister, Rita, who lived in a small apartment on Chicago's North Side.

Steinhagen's family life when she was young was considered normal, according to court psychiatric records. Walter and Edith Steinhagen had emigrated from Berlin in their early twenties, married in New York, and eventually settled in Chicago. Walter worked as a die setter and was described as a good provider; Edith, who stayed at home to care for her two daughters, always referred to Ruth as a "good girl." But in the opening sentence of the autobiography drafted for Dr. Haines, Steinhagen wrote: "In my entire life, I don't think there's ever been one thing that turned out the way I wanted it to." Rita Steinhagen said that as youngsters, she and Ruth were unhappy at school because the other children made fun of them. She always felt Ruth was more independent, but when Ruth left home and moved into her own apartment, just months before she shot Waitkus, she took a suitcase full of teddy bears and toys that she had as a child. Rita admitted to authorities that Ruth talked to her frequently about suicide but said when Ruth thought Rita was not sympathetic, she quit confiding in her.

After nearly three years in the secure culture of a state mental hospital, Steinhagen resumed life with her parents and sister amid changing family dynamics. Steinhagen's parents, who were greatly disturbed by her two-year obsession over Waitkus, became more tolerant; and in turn, Steinhagen made a serious effort to move on with her life in a positive manner. "My father is very nice and stubborn," Steinhagen said. "I am stubborn, too, that's why we don't get along. I used to get real mad and go to my room and beat my hands on the wall and then I went crazy about Eddie, and we used to fight about that." If Steinhagen was still "crazy about Eddie" when she returned home, she kept her thoughts to herself, a trait she probably learned during confinement in Kankakee.

Since her release from the state mental hospital, Steinhagen has led a secluded, private life. She has chosen to exist in the shadows of society and has made a determined and successful effort to maintain this lifestyle. There is no evidence she ever married, and as of the writing of his book, she was living with her sister, Rita, in a crowded, racially mixed section of Chicago's Northwest Side. Her home, which sits in the middle of a block of modest bungalows and apartment buildings, was originally purchased by Steinhagen and her family in 1970. Her parents, who died in the early nineties, were respected and well liked in the neighborhood.

Walter and Edith Steinhagen were very comfortable in their new home. They made friends easily, worshiped on Sundays at the nearby Lutheran church, and enjoyed the company of their neighbors. Edith had the ladies of the block to her kitchen regularly for coffee, and Walter, an expert in carpentry, helped his neighbors with home-repair projects. But their daughters, especially Ruth, who was forty when the family moved into their new neighborhood, were different. While their parents were social, Ruth and Rita, neighbors said, were quiet and withdrawn. "The parents were wonderful people, always fun-loving and happy," said Betty Jensen, who has lived a few doors from the Steinhagen home for more than thirty years. "Ever since their parents died in the early nineties, they've had very little contact with the neighbors. Rita is somewhat outgoing and pleasant, but Ruth is more private, more guarded. We don't see them much at all, except for the mornings when Rita feeds the birds in the front yard."

Another long-time resident of the block, who was a close friend of Walter and Edith Steinhagen, described Ruth and Rita as "eccentric, with peculiar beliefs." According to this neighbor, "the girls believe their parents' spirits are still with them, not in a metaphorical manner, but in a realistic way. They are very strange. I really stopped trying to talk with them anymore. I used to send them Christmas cards, because of their parents, but they never responded, so I stopped."

Steinhagen's past—her obsession with Waitkus, the shooting at the Edgewater Beach, her stay at the state mental hospital—remains hidden from her neighbors. "I really don't know about her past, you know, before they moved on this block," Jensen said. "Their parents were such nice people that I tried to get to know the girls better after their parents' deaths. I remember going to their house for coffee and recall noticing that the house was kept exactly the same way their parents kept it and very neat and clean. Both girls retired a few years ago. Ruth told me she worked in the office at a company for thirty-five years, but she never told me where she worked, and I never asked. But I don't socialize with them now; nobody does. They go out the back of the house and drive away from the garage. Sometimes they will open their front door for people, sometimes they won't. And they usually never answer the phone. We let them live the way they want, and that's it."

The profile of Steinhagen's neighborhood has changed greatly since 1970. There are only a few people on the block who knew Walter and Edith Steinhagen, and the other neighbors know nothing about their daughter, Ruth. Up and down both sides of the street the reaction to the two elderly sisters in the small, padlocked house is the same: "Ruth keeps to herself, but she is always very pleasant," her next-door neighbor said. "She's a loner-type, mostly stays in her house with her sister," a young mother said. "We really don't see them much or know anything about them," said a man who lived across the street.

Steinhagen's neighborhood has a big-city, impersonal feel to it. She lives within walking distance of the intersection of two major thoroughfares, the home to a crowded mix of businesses: fast food franchises, convenience stores, gas stations, liquor shops, and used-car lots. It is an area for transient shoppers—pull your car over, pick up a carton of cigarettes and a quart of milk, and drive away. It is not a neighborhood to linger in. Like her neighbors, business owners don't seem to know Steinhagen: "I can't recall ever seeing her, but then again we don't know the names of most of our customers around here," said the manager of a donut shop one block from Steinhagen's house. "She's never been in here," said the owner of the area's only beauty parlor. Steinhagen has had no contact with the local community center or the nearby senior citizens' club; and members of the local Lutheran church do not know her. Even the postman can't recall ever seeing her. "I drop their letters through a slot right into their house," he said. "But I never see either one of them." Steinhagen has chosen to live—and disappear—in a congested urban setting where her past and present lives will probably never meet.

Because of her continued intense desire for privacy, Steinhagen has never publicly commented about the Waitkus shooting. Over the years, reporters have sought her out for interviews, but she has always managed to avoid them. Her telephone number is unlisted, and calls to her home aren't answered with regularity. Whenever someone does make contact, Steinhagen hangs up as soon as she learns the subject of the call is related to Waitkus. Her sister, Rita, was recently asked if Ruth would talk to a writer who was working on a book on Waitkus. She became quite upset and, her voice more frightened than angry, said: "Why would you write such a book? That was a long time ago, and we want to keep it behind us. Ruth reads the sports pages every day, and this would send her back into the hospital." Before the caller could say another word, she hung up.

"Steinhagen's continued resistance to talking with anyone about the shooting or her past fits with her coherent schizophrenia," one psychiatrist suggested. "She was never disorganized. She had paranoid trends, but she obviously could communicate during the time of the shooting and afterwards. She is peculiar, guarded, but not bizarre. Many schizophrenics show obvious craziness. She didn't. She was quietly psychotic, but she felt jilted by Waitkus. Had she been more open—not hiding, for instance, when she saw Waitkus come out of the clubhouse—she maybe could have worked through the obsession without trying to kill him. If someone ever does make contact with her for an interview, I see it as a blind alley. She won't say much."

For more than five decades, Ruth Ann Steinhagen has lived a shadowy existence, trying to keep her past from reappearing. The garage door that faces the alley carries the faint stain of graffiti, and the tall oak gate leading to the property is secured with a steel padlock. It is impossible to see beyond that point because high, fortlike wood fences run along both sides of the backyard, all the way to the rear of the house. The desire for privacy of those inside dictate the home's decor: all the window's are blanketed by heavy drapery or shades; the small, diamond-shaped window on the front door is covered with a piece of plywood; a beware-of-dog sign hangs on a wire gate by the side of the small, brick-and-frame home, where an aging recluse passes the years with her sister.

14

No Sentiment in Baseball

The relationship between Waitkus and his manager had fallen apart late in the 1951 season, and they hardly spoke to each other. Sawyer complained that Waitkus kept late hours and wasn't always sharp for games. Immediately after the season, Sawyer announced that Waitkus was on the trading block; "Waitkus was a high-strung, lonesome youngster who craved company, life," Sawyer said. "He was not strong enough to keep late hours, miss his rest and play good baseball. He is anemic, takes vitamin pills regularly. Married life should make him more content, take away the tension. And he has a splendid wife who has his welfare first in her mind."

After the disastrous 1951 season, Bob Carpenter and Eddie Sawyer ran the 1952 Phillies with iron fists. They initiated an "austerity" program, which began well before spring training. When contracts were mailed out in early January, most players received healthy pay cuts ranging from 20 to 25 percent. And the austerity continued at spring training. Wives were not allowed, and all players were ordered to stay at Clearwater's Fort Harrison Hotel. There was no golf, no tennis, no swimming. Even cars were prohibited. And when Willie Jones missed a curfew, he was fined $300. "Don't you think it's time someone got tough with this team," Sawyer said. Several players objected to the new rules and reported late to camp, but Sawyer didn't care. He continued to distance himself from the players throughout the spring. If anyone had a gripe, Sawyer ordered, he was to talk to coach Cy Perkins, and Perkins would relay the message to the skipper.

In spring 1952, Waitkus found himself sharing first base with Nippy Jones, an injured utility infielder the Phillies had bought from the Cardinals organization for $10,000. Jones, who was recovering from back surgery, reported to the Phils' camp early, and that impressed Sawyer. "Jones has the [first base] job," he said. "It's up to Waitkus to take it away from him. Jones was anxious to find out if the operation on his back was successful. He wasn't due until the other infielders and outfielders were. But Jones has spirit, he wants to play ball and if he's right, he can. So he came to camp on his own time, at his own expense. Any guy, who wants to play as well as a healthy Jones can, is my guy. As of now, he's the first baseman."

In the spring of 1950, Waitkus had had to beat out Dick Sisler to keep his first base job. The following year he had been assigned to the Tom Casagrande project. Now in 1952, he had to prove himself again. "You know," he told his wife, "there's really no sentiment in baseball. It's really just a business, that's all. When you're released you get a telegram, and that's it."

Waitkus was correct. As he and Carol honeymooned in Florida, the Phillies made a surprising winter trade, dealing two players who were largely responsible for the Whiz Kids' pennant. Dick Sisler, who hit the most important home run in Phillies' history, and Andy Seminick, who played the final week of the season with a broken foot, were sent to Cincinnati, along with reserve infielder Eddie Pellagrini and rookie pitcher Niles Jordan. The Phillies got second baseman Connie Ryan, catcher Smokey Burgess, and pitcher Howie Fox.

With the Sisler and Seminick trade and all the attention being paid to Nippy Jones, it was clear Phillies management was serious about making wholesale changes. With Curt Simmons returning from the army, Carpenter tried to trade Russ Meyer and Waitkus to the Dodgers for Gil Hodges and Duke Snider. One rumor had Waitkus going to the Yankees, another to the Cardinals. "If they're going to trade me, why don't they send me to the Braves," Waitkus told Meyer, "and then I can just take the bridge across the Charles River and be home in ten minutes."

The Phillies were a disgruntled bunch when they left Florida, and they carried that sour attitude through the early part of the season. Sawyer's austerity program clearly was a mistake; the Phils lost eleven out of thirteen at one stretch from late May through early June. Nothing was working for Sawyer. Nippy Jones, his choice to replace Waitkus, never overcame his back injury and played only eight games. In late June, the Phillies lost an exhibition game to the Athletics, and Bob Carpenter had had enough. The next afternoon, after Curt Simmons shut out the Cardinals, Sawyer was fired.

"This is the first time a manager ever was fired after his club won a 6–0 shutout," Sawyer told the players.

Carpenter hired Steve O'Neill, former manager of the Indians, Tigers, and Red Sox. O'Neill inherited a 28–35 record with the Phillies, but he immediately improved the team's spirits by lifting Sawyer's restrictions. Wives, O'Neill said, could accompany their husbands on trips, the players could play cards in the clubhouse, and bed checks would be a thing of the past. The only rules—the Phillies must show proper conduct off the field and obey a sensible curfew.

Although Waitkus was happy in his new marriage, he continued to drink, especially on road trips. Quiet, sophisticated hotel bars—places like the Sheridan Plaza in Chicago and the Commodore Bar in New York—were regular stops after ball games for Waitkus and his closest pals. "Eddie was never a rowdy kind of drinker, like some players," Russ Meyer said. "He'd sit at the bar with a few of us—or by himself, it never mattered to Eddie— have his cigarettes and his drinks, and talk. Eddie could talk on any subject, and he knew what he was talking about, too. We closed plenty of bars, but Eddie never caused any trouble anywhere. Eddie even drank with class."

The drinking and the late nights, as Sawyer said, did affect Waitkus's baseball. The shooting took a toll on his body, but Waitkus didn't help himself by staying out late. He didn't have the strength to drink at night and play well the next afternoon. "He always seemed to have low energy, a real struggle for him," Carol recalled years later.

Waitkus had slumped at the plate throughout the first half of the season; his timing was off, and he was swinging at pitches he usually took for balls. But after the All Star break, O'Neill dropped Waitkus to the eighth spot in the lineup, and the move was just what Waitkus needed. He began to hit better than he had at any time since the 1950 season. "I guess eighth is my spot," Waitkus said. "I'm not as strong as some of the other men. My vitality runs low at times during the season. In eighth place, a man frequently comes to bat only three times, instead of four. He is not on the bases as often, and does not have as much running to do as a fellow in the lead-off or second spot. And it is a bit easier to hit in eighth place. You get an opportunity to take a crack at the 3–0 and 3–1 pitch more often, because the pitcher, who usually is not a dangerous hitter, follows. So the opposing pitcher occasionally relaxes and gives you the soft one. I hope I continue to bat eighth. I'm happy there."

O'Neill led the Phils to a 59–32 record and a respectable fourth-place finish. After his slow start, Waitkus finished the season with a .289 average, 144 hits, twenty-nine doubles, and forty-nine runs batted in. He played in 146 games; the only games he missed were early in the season when Sawyer experimented with Nippy Jones. "What a job Waitkus did for me," O'Neill said.

During the final few weeks of the season, however, Waitkus developed a severe cold that settled in his chest. For days he ran a temperature of 100 degrees, and he received daily shots of penicillin. But he played every day, and actually developed a more powerful swing, driving the ball to deep parts of the outfield. He only hit two home runs and four triples, but the ball came off his bat with more authority. "The man may be the 'new' Eddie Waitkus," Stan Baumgartner wrote in the *Bulletin*. "It would be an astonishing role—a complete turnaround, a Jekyll-Hyde transformation."

Waitkus had his own explanation for his strong late-season play in 1952. He said a doctor told him: "Those things happen. We saw many cases like that in war time. Sometimes a soldier who was wounded came through hospitalization okay and was sent back to his unit. Then all of a sudden he came apart again. Some other officers thought guys like that were 'goldbricking.' But the fellow was actually suffering from 'delayed shock.' That's what happened to you, Eddie. You thought you were okay, and I guess you were. Then came the let-down. You're lucky you beat it."

"I think the doctor was right," Waitkus said. "This is the first year since 1949 that I've felt well and strong and able to play nine innings. This whole year was a challenge to me. When we arrived in training camp, I was told that I had to beat out Nippy Jones for my job. I wasn't afraid of that challenge, provided my health and stamina stayed with me. I really didn't recover from that bullet wound in Chicago until last year. Then came the excitement and pressure of winning the pennant and playing the World Series. In 1951, I had an awful letdown. Our trainer called it 'delayed reaction.' I had a terrible year. It wasn't until after Carol and I were married that things started to work out right. Now I'm myself again." His marriage to Carol had shaped his life in a positive way. "No more late night card playing with the boys," one reporter wrote. "Since Carol Waitkus came into the picture, Eddie has been a different person. He has the ability. She supplies the drive and inspiration."

By the end of the 1952 season, Carol was pregnant with their first child. In late fall Waitkus, who had a morning and afternoon radio program on WPTR in Albany, surprised her with an anniversary gift. On a cold November morning, accompanied by a musical background of "My Foolish Heart," Waitkus, in a soft Boston accent, shared their story with his listeners:

Today is a special day. Our story for this morning is not only a sports story, but also a love story. It shows that sometimes truth is stranger than fiction.

In 1949, a first-baseman of the Philadelphia Phillies was shot by a deranged girl. For weeks he hovered between life and death. After his release he was called into the Phillies office and told that he was being sent to Clearwater, Florida, with the club trainer to take the one-in-a-thousand chance that he might recover enough to stand the competition of big league baseball.

A grueling schedule laid out for him the first few weeks was a nightmare, and the ballplayer, already in a bad nervous condition from his accident, grew more depressed and reluctant to go on each day. He was tempted to give up the whole ordeal and the game of baseball that meant so much to him.

Then he met a girl. A girl who knew nothing of baseball. Their few hellos on the beaches grew to infrequent dates. Slowly he started to withdraw from his shell and lose the fear he had developed of people. Slowly, through her influence, he started to take interest again in the world around him. And with her quiet confidence to help him, he went into his training with renewed interest. She had faith that he could come back, so he had to do it for her sake.

When the going got rough, she was always there to cheer him on. When he felt like quitting, she was there to prod him on. The months went on, and spring training started with another battle to face . . . the battle to regain his job. He did, and with her comforting presence in the background, went on to a great season and a World Series.

That year the newspapers called his the "Comeback of the Year." But he didn't do it alone. The season ended and the companionship grew into something deeper. As happens in your fiction, they were married and went back into baseball together.

That music you hear in the background was their particular song, and today is their anniversary. As you see, it's not only a sports story, but the story behind an athletic figure. It's the story of how a woman's influence, and a woman's inspiration, helped a man fight the greatest battle of his life. It's the story of all the women behind all the men.

A story as old as time.

Waitkus was a happy man that winter; he was comfortable in his marriage, he was about to become a father, and he was feeling healthy. But Waitkus would begin the next baseball season unsure of his role with the Phillies. Shortly after taking over as Phillies manager, O'Neill had an on-field run-in with Russ Meyer that eventually had an impact on Waitkus. Meyer was coasting with a 6–0 lead against the Boston Braves one afternoon when he suddenly lost his control and walked five straight batters. An irritated O'Neill ordered a coach to go to the mound to pull Meyer. But when Eddie Mayo asked for the ball, Meyer turned his back. O'Neill was livid. He jumped out of the dugout, raced across the infield, and tore the ball from the pitcher's hand. A resentful O'Neill traded Meyer after the season in a three-way deal with the Braves and Dodgers. In the deal the Phillies acquired first baseman Earl Torgeson, one of Waitkus's closest friends from his minor league days.

On the first day of spring camp in 1953, with Waitkus still back home in Albany, O'Neill said: "Earl Torgeson will start at first base, and if he responds the way I expect, Eddie Waitkus will be traded." Once again, Waitkus began a spring with someone poised to grab his job, this time one of his closest friends. Waitkus's mind, however, wasn't entirely on baseball when O'Neill made his comments, because on February 19, Carol delivered a baby girl, Veronica, named after Waitkus's mother.

After weeks of haggling with Bob Carpenter over his contract, Waitkus finally signed and reported to camp in late March. "I had to sign before [Robin] Roberts so there would be some money left," he said. "I have an heir now." Waitkus's salary was $17,500, and a "special covenants" clause in his standard player's contract called for him to receive an extra $500 if the Phillies home attendance exceeded 950,000. When Waitkus arrived in Clearwater, Carpenter told him: "Before you put on your uniform, I want you to understand that your contract is not on the market this moment. Everyone knows that I have two first basemen, you and Torgy, and I will be asked to make deals. That doesn't mean, however, that I will make one."

Waitkus didn't want to be traded, but he did want to play regularly. He knew Torgeson's fielding at first base couldn't compare to his, but Torgeson gave the Phillies power from the left side. "No owner is going to carry a couple of guys like Torgeson and me," Waitkus said. "He's a wonderful guy, a friend of long standing, and a swell ball player. Since he can hit home runs more often than I can, I suppose he's more certain of his job with the Phillies than I am. Once you decide to play baseball for a living you've got to expect these things, but I've never been so happy playing ball as I have been since Steve O'Neill took the club. Any guy who can't play for O'Neill should get another kind of job."

Waitkus went about his business that spring, played a great first base, and was strong at the plate. In late March, a few days before O'Neill announced he would start Torgeson on opening day, Waitkus put on quite a display in Lakeland, Florida, against the Washington Senators. He went three-for-four, scored a run, and made two sensational plays at first base. Still a very popular player, especially in the relaxed spring training atmosphere, the crowd roared with approval on each play Waitkus made at first, especially late in the game when he snared Connie Ryan's wild throw to complete the Phillies' third double play of the game.

"Eddie, you look like a guy who's got a family to support," Russ Meyer, who watched the game from the stands, told him.

"There's an old saying about 'hanging in there,' Russ," Waitkus said. "Ever hear of it?"

"Yeh, but don't pop off about it. I learned my lesson. Since I went to Brooklyn, I've kept my yap shut and done just what I was supposed to do. Let the other guys pop off."

The season of 1953 was dismal for Waitkus, from start to finish. He played in only eighty-one games, and although he hit .291 and .400 as a pinch hitter, tops in the league, Waitkus was upset about sharing first base with Torgeson. Although Waitkus was a left-handed batter, O'Neill used him almost exclusively against left-handed pitching and played Torgeson, who also hit left-handed, against right-handers. Waitkus resented this, saying his average would be much higher if he were allowed to bat against right-handed pitching. "Sitting on the bench is no good for me," he complained. Waitkus became morose and disinterested. Carpenter placed his name on the waiver list several times, but Waitkus never cleared the National League. The Phillies wanted to make a deal with an American League team, but each National League team first had to pass on Waitkus.

Hank Greenberg, general manager of Cleveland, told O'Neill, "Get Waitkus out of the National League and we'll give you what you need." The Indians were interested in sending an aging Bob Feller to the Phillies for Waitkus. Carpenter also had his eye on young Harvey Kuenn of Detroit.

"I'm a ball player, and ball clubs have the right to trade a player anywhere they want," Waitkus told the press. "I do hope, though, to play regularly wherever I am this year." But the trading deadline passed unceremoniously, and Eddie Waitkus remained a Phillie.

Waitkus's resentment at not playing regularly ate at him as the season wore on. As always, he displayed a cool professionalism on the field, and he kept his excellent rapport with teammates and reporters. But he fumed inside. As his tension grew, so did his postgame stays at the bar in Philadelphia's Warwick Hotel. The less he played, the more depressed he became, and the more he drank. "The last few years he played baseball were very tough on Eddie, mentally and physically," Carol recalled years later. "He'd have drinks to pick himself up. Eddie used alcohol to self-medicate."

Waitkus's emotions toward the end of the season were unstable and fragile, and his drinking didn't help. In late September, with the Phillies battling for third place, Waitkus's tension—and drinking life—got the best of him. Following a long session at a New York bar, Waitkus jumped the team and took a train to Boston to visit his father. Waitkus never asked for permission to leave and never offered an explanation; he said later he was battling "end-of-the-season nerves" and needed to see his ailing father. Stephen Waitkus, however, was in good health when Waitkus arrived at the family's Melrose home. "Eddie and I had our differences the last year I managed the Phillies," Eddie Sawyer said decades later, "but Waitkus was the last guy you'd figure would jump the team. Eddie was battling a lot of demons the last few years he played baseball, and his drinking didn't help his mental state at all. We all knew it at the time. Looking back, I guess we should had tried to help him, but then again most ballplayers drank in those days. With Eddie, though, you got the sense there was something more going on inside him than just the drinking."

Carpenter was furious with Waitkus. He reached him by phone and the two men exchanged heated words. Following the conversation, Carpenter suspended Waitkus for the remainder of the season and docked him eight days' pay. "What else was there to do?" Carpenter said. "He was under contract to play until the end of the season. If he wants to jump the club and run his own affairs I certainly am not going to pay him, and he was told he was not welcome back on the team. Sure he's a good ball player, but he doesn't want to play for us the way we want him to play. So there's nothing left to do but let him go to the highest bidder."

Waitkus was conciliatory, but he offered no real justification for leaving his team. "My imagination was working overtime and I made a mistake," he said. "They were perfectly justified in suspending me." He later confided to Meyer: "I think I better get back to Albany and think things over. Maybe I'm at an age when I should think about ending baseball."

The following February, Carpenter, who had officially lifted the suspension, sent Waitkus a contract for the 1954 season; it included a healthy pay cut. Waitkus sent back the pact and scribbled: "N.S.F.—"Not Sufficient Funds" on the front of the contract. He also enclosed a personal letter to Carpenter, apologizing for his actions at the close of the season. While he never revealed what was in the letter, he told his friend Frank Yeutter: "I do a lot of screwy things, and nine times out of ten, I'm sorry for them afterward. This was one of those nine times. I was in a terrible state of mind. I wasn't playing. My father was really pretty sick and all I got from family was evasive answers. The season was almost over. We were in New York. My father was in Boston. So I figured to myself, 'What's the use of stalling around here, I'm not helping anyone.' So I took off. No one could blame Bob for punishing me. I didn't, at any rate. You've got to respect his sincerity in everything he does. He wants a winning ball club, and he'll spend all kinds of money to get it. He's been pretty good to all of us. He saved my life when I ran into that shooting accident in Chicago."

Waitkus balked at two contracts before finally signing, and when he arrived at Clearwater weeks later, he realized Carpenter meant it when he said he'd let Waitkus "go to the highest bidder." O'Neill didn't play Waitkus in a single exhibition game, and this enraged him. A few days before the end of the exhibition season, Waitkus spotted Carpenter in the outfield during warm-ups. He raced across Athletic Field and shouted at his boss: "Why haven't I been in one game, Bob? Not one game."

"Why? I'll tell you why," Carpenter shot back. "Because you've just been sold to the Baltimore Orioles. That's why." With that, Carpenter turned and walked away, and Waitkus's tenure with the Philadelphia Phillies ended. Carpenter had sold Waitkus for $40,000 to the American League Orioles.

Packing his duffel bag in the Phillies' Clearwater clubhouse, the thirty-four-year-old Waitkus told an ex-teammate, "See that old glove? It is sort of beat up, just like me. But I think we're both good for a few more years. That's about what it amounts to. But let's be practical about it, over there

I can play almost every day; here I was with the scrubeenies. But I've got no hard feelings. Everyone has been real swell to me."

Waitkus was by far the most popular first baseman on the Philadelphia Phillies. "Having Waitkus and Torgeson was tough on both Torgeson and me," O'Neill said after Waitkus left the club. "No matter how well Torgeson played, no matter how well he hit, he never could become a favorite with Philadelphia fans as long as Waitkus was around. I have seen Torgeson make two hits on his first two times up and not get even a ripple of applause from the fans. But if he made an error later the fans would ride him and shout for Waitkus."

Waitkus didn't want to leave Philadelphia, but his desire to play every day led him to become optimistic about Baltimore. "I am sorry to leave for sentimental reasons," he said. "I've made a lot of friends in Philadelphia and some of my happiest memories are woven around the pennant we won in 1950. In five years it seems everything has happened to me. But you can't let sentiment interfere with your well being, and a man can't make much money sitting on the bench—or trying to share a first baseman's salary with someone else. Sitting on the bench last season drove me crazy. It was like sitting on cloud '13' in the sky, waiting for lightning to strike. I don't know anything about the American League, and my little black book on the National League pitchers won't help me over there. But I'll keep pinging away, trying to make singles as I did here."

Hours after he was sold to the Orioles, the Fort Harrison Hotel in Clearwater hosted a lavish end-of-spring-training cocktail party and buffet supper for the players and club officials. "How do you like my farewell party?" Waitkus quipped to everyone. "That's old Eddie, first cabin all the way." Bob Carpenter's wife, Mary, then offered a toast to "the nicest guy on the ball club."

15

A Quiet Existence

You see, I've always sort of looked upon baseball as something akin to show business," Waitkus said, just prior to his debut with the Baltimore Orioles. "Ninety-five per cent of the players you see have an actor's temperament—we're extroverts and we like to be appreciated. And me? I hate to get left out of any act. That's why it's nice to be with Baltimore. Last year was a nightmare for me. Sometimes I felt like I was slowly going berserk. It was an awful feeling sitting on the bench after being in there day after day all those years. I just couldn't adjust myself to it. You've got to play regularly in this game in order to make a decent living. I'm sure I'm going to like it in Baltimore. This city is all excited about getting into the majors and it should prove to be very interesting. The thing I like best, however, is that I'm getting a chance to play. That's all I ask."

Waitkus joined his new team in late March in Mesa, Arizona, where the Orioles were playing the Cubs in a spring training game. Baltimore was managed by Jimmie Dykes, who boasted that his infield was potentially one of the best in the majors. "When Eddie Waitkus gets in shape we'll have one of the finest glove men in the game at first base," Dykes said. "Bobby Young is the sparkplug of the team at second. Bill Hunter is everything we thought he was at shortstop, and Junior Stephens is beginning to 'find himself' at third."

The first thing Waitkus did when he met the Orioles at Rendezvous Park was run twelve laps around the outfield. He told Dykes that he had little opportunity to run at the Phillies' camp because of a National League rule prohibiting legwork in the outfield while games were being played. Waitkus also spent much time in the batting cage, trying to regain his timing after spending the spring in Clearwater sitting on the bench. In his first game with the Orioles, Waitkus impressed everyone with his fielding, especially the Baltimore baseball writers. "Heady Eddie made a five inning debut in Sunday's 8–2 loss to the Cubs, the last time the Flock played, and on one difficult chance, a twisting bouncer over the bag, slapped his glove on the spheroid with the finality of a bug collector bagging a butterfly," James Ellis wrote in the *Baltimore Sun*.

Hours after the Orioles purchased Waitkus, their first baseman, Dick Kryhoski, broke his wrist when he was hit by a pitched ball during a game. Kryhoski, a power hitter who was a favorite of Dykes, missed the first few weeks of the season. The injury to Kryhoski allowed Waitkus to start the season at first base with no competition. But the year began miserably for him. He hit only .170, and Kryhoski replaced him in the lineup in early May. But Kryhoski also struggled, and Dykes brought Waitkus back to first base after two weeks. He stormed back with a home run against the Yankees, and by early June, Waitkus was hitting .290. "He has really given us a lift," Dykes said. "Eddie was handicapped at the beginning of the season by not getting enough work from his old club. A fellow getting up in age needs to work to stay in top shape. He's getting back to his old form." Kryhoski also had praise for Waitkus. "Sure, I'd like to get back in there," he said, "but the other guy is playing good ball. I'll have to wait."

In early June, the Orioles visited Boston, and Waitkus finally had a chance to play a major league game in Fenway Park. "Eddie Waitkus was my idol," said George Sullivan, author and veteran Boston baseball writer. "When the Orioles made their first trip to Boston in '54, I interviewed Waitkus for the *Cambridge Chronicle*. I was a kid reporter and Waitkus was a legend in Cambridge, and it was a thrill for me to talk with him. Eddie, I remember, was pretty sentimental and he felt like reminiscing about the old days. He talked about his high school coach, Sonny Foley, about the Frisoli club, and about Jack Burns and Cambridge Field. 'We certainly had a lot of fun with baseball in those days,' he told me."

Waitkus also talked to Sullivan about the shooting at the Edgewater Beach and his war years, and he offered some insight into how those experiences affected his emotional state. He said he was amazed at the irony of being shot in a hotel room by a teenage girl after surviving heavy combat in World War II. Waitkus also admitted he still had trouble sleeping at night and wondered when, if ever, he would be able to clear his mind of the shooting at the Edgewater Beach and his war experience in the Pacific. He told Sullivan he was reminded of this whenever he came to the ballpark: "Each time someone steps on an empty paper cup and it makes a loud pop, I want to hit the deck, especially during batting practice when the park is empty."

Fenway Park proved to be unlucky for Waitkus. In the opener of a doubleheader, he twisted his foot rounding second base; X-rays showed no break, but the foot was badly swollen. Waitkus missed the next two weeks, and Dykes replaced him once again with Kryhoski, who went on a fifteen-game hitting streak. Dykes alternated between Waitkus and Kryhoski for the rest of the 1954 season. The Orioles were playing well during the middle of the year and had moved into fifth place in the league. "All I ask when I'm sitting in the dugout is that the fellows win," Waitkus said. "I've ridden the bench before, but it really gets darn lonesome sitting there when the club is getting beat. Nobody wants to talk to you."

Waitkus's role with his new team wasn't all he'd hoped for. He played in only ninety-five games for the Orioles in 1954 and hit a respectable .283; his fielding percentage was a flashy 1.000, not one error in seventy-eight games at first base. The Orioles, though, were looking for young players. Paul Richards replaced Dykes as the new manager of the Orioles in 1955, and he was intent on rebuilding the team, which lost one hundred games and finished fifty-seven games behind league-leading Cleveland the previous season. The Orioles went on a spending spree, signing a string of bonus babies, including Brooks Robinson, who remembered Waitkus this way: "Eddie came to Baltimore with a great fielding reputation. Even then, very late in his career, he had a sweet swing, very fluid, very easy, much like Tony Gwynn. And he was outstanding at first base. I'll always remember Eddie as being very friendly, always well dressed, and a very classy player."

Although very popular with his teammates, Waitkus was never truly happy in Baltimore. He called his stay there "a strange experience." His health and emotional state were slipping, and Waitkus's days in baseball appeared to be numbered. His back hurt more each day, and while he and Carol enjoyed their home life with two-year-old Veronica, Waitkus was upset with what he thought was a very chaotic Orioles organization. As he had in Philadelphia, he drank quietly and brooded about not playing regularly.

Waitkus signed his 1955 contract with the Orioles in mid-January for $14,000, the same salary he'd received the year before. "I was cursed with being a good defensive man and a light hitter," he said. "That's why I drive a low-priced car instead of a big limousine." While the Baltimore management was committed to a youth movement, Richards, who Waitkus said "was a great manager" and "miles ahead of most managers," did not want to simply discard a veteran like Waitkus. But his team needed to stay within a twenty-five-man roster, so they placed Waitkus on the Disabled List; this way they could maintain possession of him and adhere to the player limit. The Orioles announced that Waitkus had a sore back, and they kept him on the DL longer than the thirty-day minimum. Waitkus, however, worked out daily with the team at home and on the road. "Actually, there was never anything wrong with me, except maybe my disposition," he said. "I'd go out to the ball park and work out. Then I'd have to dress and go up into the stands to watch the game." Richards loved Waitkus's defensive ability, but he liked the home run power of Gus Triandos better. Waitkus was clearly expendable as a member of the 1955 Baltimore Orioles.

Although he never admitted it in public, his back was giving him trouble. Adhesions in his lower back muscles, caused by the surgery to remove the bullet, plagued him for years. He also continued to drink, and he found it very difficult to stay in top condition, especially for day games. "It was really hard for him those last few seasons," Carol recalled. "He always had a tough time exercising his back, and his energy level was very low. Eddie would get to the ballpark by three in the afternoon for a night game and spend as much time as he could in the whirlpool."

Because of the never-ending personnel changes with the Orioles, Waitkus called his Baltimore experience "a madhouse." The organization was in a constant search to find new talent. Each day, it seemed, someone was trying out for the team, or some young player would be signing a hearty bonus. "We had three teams in Baltimore," Waitkus said. "We had one team going, one team playing, and one team coming in. For me, I sat on the bench so long I wore a groove in the lumber."

When the Orioles traveled to Boston in July, Waitkus once again spent some time with George Sullivan, who found his Cambridge idol to be much more sullen and cynical than the year before. Jack Burns, Waitkus's Cambridge Field mentor, was starting his first year as a third base coach for the Red Sox in 1955, and the Boston-Baltimore series that year marked the first and only times that Burns and Waitkus appeared on the same major league diamond. Sullivan talked with Waitkus in the Orioles' dugout before the first game of the series. The youthful reporter wanted to know Waitkus's thoughts about young baseball players and the opportunities that exist in organized baseball. Waitkus commented on all the money the Orioles were giving to young talent right out of high school and college. "No doubt about it," he said, "opportunity is at its highest peak now. And all the youngster has to do is play, play and play some more." Waitkus then grabbed his glove and started to step out of the dugout when he turned and told Sullivan, "But if the youngsters really want some good advice, tell them to buy a math book and go to MIT. This life murders you."

Waitkus played in only thirty-eight games for the Orioles. He hit .259, had only two extra-base hits, and scored just two runs. In late July, the Orioles handed Waitkus his unconditional release, and a few days later, he signed with the Phillies. Waitkus caught up with his old team for a road game in Cincinnati, and he singled as a pinch hitter. Philadelphia, however, wasn't much different than Baltimore for Waitkus, who saw his career ending. He played in thirty-three games for the Phillies and hit .280. On a brisk, late-September evening in Brooklyn, Eddie Waitkus played his final major league game. His back aching with every stretch at first base, he worked both ends of a twi-night doubleheader at Ebbets Field, where five years earlier he had scored the winning run in the Whiz Kids' dramatic pennant victory. The Phillies lost both games. But in the seventh inning of the opener, Waitkus stepped to the plate and hit a home run off Don Newcombe. After crossing home plate, he stepped out of character when he tipped his hat to Carol, who sat with friends behind the Philadelphia dugout. From the Dodgers' bullpen, Russ Meyer watched his old friend and smiled.

On October 6, 1955, a telegram arrived at 8 Circle Lane in Albany, New York. The Phillies had given Waitkus his unconditional release. After 1,140 major league games, Eddie Waitkus was out of baseball at the age of thirty-six. Like most players of his era, Waitkus's last major league game placed him on a threshold where he had to begin yet another new life without baseball. Waitkus had never made—or saved—enough money to retire, so when his baseball days came to an end, the problem he faced was making a living and letting go of the past. He also had his pride. "What's the use of battering around a baseball when you know your days are numbered?" Waitkus asked. "I might be able to get another year in the majors. Then it becomes a matter of trying to catch on as a coach in the majors, or playing a couple of more years in the Coast League or Triple-A minors. That's not for me. I was a big leaguer and I'm going out a big leaguer."

Waitkus's body was tired when he left the game. The muscles in his back ached daily and he did not have the stamina—physically or mentally—for another long season of baseball. Drinking, Waitkus said often, was not a problem as long as he worked out regularly and stayed in shape. But his drinking escalated in a world without baseball, and it quickly shaped his personal life.

Waitkus really had no plans for his professional life after baseball. He and Carol spent the fall of 1955 discussing options, including an offer to work for Carol's uncle, who owned a beer distribution business. Waitkus politely declined. "I want to go it on my own," he told his wife. In mid-November, Waitkus attended a speaking engagement in New York, where he met up with retired New York Yankee first baseman Buddy Hassett. The two men had a few beers together after their speeches, and Waitkus told Hassett he had decided to "hang 'em up." Hassett, a vice president of sales with Eastern Freightways, a New Jersey–based trucking firm, promptly threw an offer his way. "Let's talk about a job then," he said. "We can use a guy like you."

A few weeks later, Eastern made a job offer, and Waitkus started with the trucking firm at the end of January. Waitkus attended classes for the first few weeks to become familiar with the traffic pattern between Phila-delphia and Buffalo, his assigned territory. He began his new career in sales and public relations with a good attitude. "Sure I'm going to miss playing baseball," he said, "but for once I'll be able to live a sensible home life. I'll have a lot of fun sitting in the grandstand second-guessing every manager in the majors. And nobody will call me a 'clubhouse lawyer.' I'll be a grand-stand attorney." Carol was confident her husband would survive away from the game. "It's difficult for everybody to leave baseball, but Eddie was not a person whose whole life was wrapped up in just baseball," she said. "Eddie liked being a baseball player, but he never fed off the adulation. He never felt that because he was out of baseball his life was not rich."

Waitkus just couldn't walk away from the Phillies without formally saying good-bye. When the 1956 Philadelphia Phillies arrived at spring camp, a hand-written note was pinned to the clubhouse bulletin board:

Dear Robin [Roberts] and ex-teammates:

It was too big a job to write to all of you individually last fall, so I thought I had better wait until the troops were congregated in the training camp to bid my farewell, and to say thanks.

You'll find that no matter how many teams you play with in baseball, there is always one whose members are closer, and with whom you seem to share a lot more. It was that way between your old dad and the Whiz Kids. It's something I'll never forget.

After I serve my apprenticeship, I'll be in Philadelphia permanently and I'll be seeing you from the other side of the scene. My sincere best wishes to you individually and as a team.

Have a helluva season, and remember you have one fan—win, lose or draw.

Eddie

Eastern Freightways was yet another new journey for Waitkus, one he took with a growing family. On September 9, 1956, five days after Waitkus turned thirty-seven, Carol gave birth to a baby boy, Edward Waitkus Jr. Shortly after his first birthday, Waitkus nicknamed his son "Sputnik" after the Soviet Union's space satellite. Waitkus's sister, Stella Kasperwicz, said, "The happiest time in his life was when he was married, with his children." Eastern Freightways gave Waitkus a good salary and a stable work environment, but he had a very hard time adjusting to a world away from baseball. "The job was very tough for Eddie," Carol said. "There were always hassles over unions and management, things Eddie didn't really know. And sales wasn't his thing. He was comfortable in his own group, but not as a salesman. He really got the job because of his name."

The more Waitkus realized he wasn't comfortable in his new work environment, the more he turned to alcohol. In June 1957, Eastern transferred Waitkus to Buffalo, and although he and Carol enjoyed the locale, their relationship slowly started to unwind. Carol stayed at home, cared for their two young children, and attended some college classes, while her husband tried to hang on to a job he hated. His depression worsened, he became less and less communicative at home, and his drinking increased. "We lived a very quiet existence in Buffalo," Carol said. "Eddie was becoming very depressed, and we didn't go out much. Buffalo is where I saw Eddie's drinking escalate, in a very quiet way. Eddie's drinking was never all that visible. He was never abusive, never stayed out late at night, always came home.

But he was noncommunicative, and he always felt he needed a drink to pick himself up."

Waitkus was a retired athlete, but he was much more than just an ex–major leaguer. He had a wife and children he adored; he was a voracious reader, usually books about history, especially the Civil War and World War II; and he loved poetry, often reading to his children. But something was missing. "Dad was a poet," his daughter, Ronni, recalled. "He expressed his feelings so well, and his writing was wonderful, but because he was such a private man, keeping so much inside, I never knew if what he wrote was his true feelings or not. I don't feel I'm able to pass on to my kids anything about my father."

"Rather than seeking the treatment he needed, Eddie self-medicated with alcohol to ease his depression," Carol said years later. The quiet, solitary drinking consumed his personality and threatened his marriage and his livelihood. Waitkus, once a glib, young baseball player, sank deeper into himself—and his past—as he approached middle age. "I remember as a kid, my dad would put me on his lap and spin his 1945 Cubs National League championship ring around my small finger," Ted Waitkus said. "He cherished that ring, and he used to tell me, 'Son I don't have much, but when I die, this is yours.'"

For the first time in his life, Eddie Waitkus refused to come back. He lacked the stamina to shape his life without baseball. His job with Eastern Freightways suffered, and his marriage slowly crumbled. He began to fall apart inwardly, but he remained the cool professional. Except for his wife, most people could not read his emotions. "The company sent me out to Buffalo to keep an eye on Eddie for a while," Buddy Hassett said. "His job performance was slipping so they wanted me to check on him. I spent a week with Eddie and his family, and to be honest, I really didn't see anything wrong with him. He was drinking some, but I didn't think it was anything serious."

There was a void in his life, according to his wife, but Waitkus could never tell anyone what it was; he probably didn't know himself. Late in his life, Waitkus told his son, "When you're playing baseball and working out every day, the drinking isn't a problem because you're in shape." It may not have been, but it was a problem after baseball, when he searched to find a new direction. And his refusal to seek help forced yet another turn in his life; Eddie Waitkus, once a victim of fate, was now becoming a victim of himself.

In 1960, the Waitkuses separated. When Ronni was seven years old and Ted four, Carol moved to Albany to be with her family. "This is not an 'I'm leaving you kind of thing,'" she told him. She did not file for divorce at the time, hoping he would find his way on his own. Shortly after the separation, Eastern officials transferred Waitkus to Camden, New Jersey, thinking a change of locale might help his morale and job performance. But away from his family, his state of mind—and his drinking—only worsened. Waitkus was barely hanging on to his job—and his sanity. In late February, 1961, after suffering what doctors called "a mild nervous disorder," Waitkus was admitted to the Veterans Administration hospital in Philadelphia. His friend, Frank Yeutter, reported Waitkus "suffered a debilitating nervous breakdown."

The stress of performing in a job he hated certainly added to Waitkus's mental breakdown. He worked long hours, and he was trying to survive in a world that was completely foreign to him. And when he tried to cope without his family, he cracked. But there were other issues that contributed to his fall. "I don't think he was a manic depressive," Carol said. "But he was always depressed but could never explain why. Drinking, too, was a problem, and the V.A. hospital never really picked up on it. He never came to terms with either problem."

Waitkus was still very popular in Philadelphia, and he wanted to tell everyone he was really okay, just a little tired from work. He told Yeutter, "It was too much for me. I tried to do too much and didn't give my body a chance to rest. My mind told my body what to do but the flesh wasn't up to the mission. So I landed here in this 'Kookie Council.' I'm not violent, I don't see strange animals. I'm not going to jump out a window. I'm here because I need a rest and get my mind off business for a while. One doctor studies this and another studies that. They're trying to find out if anything happened to me in the past that may affect me now." Waitkus told Yeutter there were other factors in his past that had led to his breakdown. He believed he had built up nervous tension for years ever since the shooting in the Edgewater Beach Hotel. Waitkus also thought his extensive combat experience in World War II—and the stress of trying to return as a top ballplayer—added to his tension. "Something had to give," he said.

Waitkus was always very smart with reporters. He wanted Yeutter to get the word out that he was interested in getting back into baseball. "I thought the business world was going to be just fine. It is so far as the money is concerned. But I worry too much. I want to do everything at once. I'd be better off if I were a minor league manager or major league coach. Baseball was my first love." Lying in his hospital bed with his future unclear, Waitkus took comfort in baseball. "What a year," he told Yeutter. "What a wonderful gang. I'll never forget that first day of October in 1950 when Dick Sisler's home run in the 10th inning won the pennant. Do you know that the run I scored from second base was actually the winning run?"

Waitkus spent several days at the Philadelphia V.A. hospital. He took tranquilizers to ease his anxiety, and doctors questioned Eddie about his past to see if there was any connection to his nervous disorder. But, according to Carol, they never really hit on the problem, and Waitkus never followed up with psychological counseling following his release. And he never returned to Eastern Freightways. Instead, he took an apartment in Philadelphia and found a job on the sales floor at Wanamakers department store.

16

Hidden Enemy

Often overlooked because of the trauma of the Edgewater Beach shooting was the psychological impact of the war years on Eddie Waitkus. World War II took three baseball seasons from Waitkus, but it affected his entire life. "He talked more about the war than he did about baseball," his wife, Carol, said.

Waitkus had just turned twenty-four when he left for the war and was engaged in some of the fiercest battles in the Pacific theater. He fought in the final, crucial stages of General Douglas MacArthur's island-hopping offensive, Operation Cartwheel. Its mission: cut off Tokyo from its southeast Asian empire and provide MacArthur with a triumphant return to the Philippines. Involved in the western prong of Cartwheel, Waitkus faced fanatical Japanese resistance, grueling jungle terrain, and horrid conditions. He experienced firsthand the horrors of war: he survived kamikaze attacks on Navy ships; nausea and artillery fire in crowded, rocking assault boats; bloody beachheads strewn with dead soldiers; machine, artillery, and mortar fire from maniacal Japanese defenders; oppressive heat, malaria, and maddening tropical flies; endless months of C rations; and the always present stench of death from nearby foxholes. Waitkus's innocence was lost forever in the twisted jungles of the Pacific, and he carried this trauma with him for the rest of his life.

By mid-September 1944, Waitkus was part of a task force of one hundred ships carrying forty thousand troops. This offensive drove up the north coast of New Guinea and crossed the equator into the northern hemisphere, headed for Morotai, a small, palm-fringed island between New Guinea and the Philippines. Morotai was used by General MacArthur as an advance base for liberating the Philippines. The goal was to clear the island of the Japanese military and establish an airfield for the army air force to use as a staging base for Cartwheel's next objective—Mindanao, the southernmost large island in the Philippines. From Morotai, Waitkus's unit joined the Thirty-seventh Infantry Division for combat operations in Bougainville, in the Solomon Islands. And in late October, Waitkus joined the Fourteenth Corps of the Sixth Army for General MacArthur's final assault in liberating the Philippines.

Sergeant Angelo Dolce and Corporal Eddie Waitkus were always together. They fought by each other's side, from island to island, all the way to Japan. They returned home together and made plans to continue their friendship stateside. From his Brooklyn home, Angelo Dolce was forever haunted by his World War II combat experience. "It's very hard to sleep nights, even today. When you remember what we all went through, it's still painful, even after all these years. I guess Ed had the same problem." After more than fifty years, Angelo still struggled with his wartime memories but agreed to relate some of the combat he experienced with Waitkus.

The Landing on Morotai. "We were lucky to reach the beach alive. We got in under heavy fire, and Ed and I quickly dug out a foxhole in the dark. The Japanese were dug into caves, natural bunkers in the jungles, and they came out at night—like maniacs—with all kinds of firepower. Mortar shells were exploding all around us in the night, and the Japanese were tossing hand grenades near us. One landed near our foxhole, exploding by one of our guys, Ed Schultz. We heard him screaming in pain. Ed Waitkus left the relative safety of our foxhole in the black of night to see what he could do for Schultz. This was the kind of soldier, the kind of person, Waitkus was, especially in the heat of battle. The explosion ripped open a long, ten-inch gash in Schultz's leg. Ed couldn't stop the bleeding, and all the time Schultz won't stop crying and screaming. Ed always thought well in crucial situations; he found some safety pins from Schultz's gear and closed the wound in the dark and saved Schultz's life. I've always thought Ed should have received a medal for what he did under fire to save Ed Schultz."

Bougainville, the Solomons. "We were under heavy mortar and rifle fire right from the initial landing and every day after that. There were Japanese planes all across the sky, dropping bombs as we prepared to hit the shore. We were in an amphibious landing vehicle, number 426. I still remember the number. With fire and smoke all around us, and the vehicle bouncing up and down in the heavy waves, Ed yelled, 'We're sitting ducks, and we're going to get hit by a shell.' So Ed and I jumped from the craft and hit the water just before number 426 received a direct hit. There were two guys left in the amp; they didn't know what hit them. If it weren't for Ed's quick thinking, we could have been dead before we hit the beach. When we got to the beach, there were so many wounded and dead soldiers lying everywhere, bodies floating in the water, bodies stacked and twisted all over the sand. I'll never forget that sight. It will be in my dreams forever. I'm sure Ed never forgot that beach and all its death."

The Philippines. "We were in the initial waves on the assault at Lingayen Gulf [January 9, 1945], a huge operation. Although we had the honor to be on the beach at Leyte Gulf [October 23–27, 1944] when General MacArthur stepped off his LCM [landing craft mechanized] in the water and got his feet wet to be with his men, we were constantly under heavy fire at Lingayen Gulf. Even before we lowered ourselves to the assault boats, we had to survive Japanese kamikaze suicide planes that crashed into other ships in the huge flotilla. When we finally reached the beach, Japanese planes filled the sky and were dropping bombs and machine gun fire. From the beach, we fought our way by motor convoy to Manila Bay, the Wall City. The fighting was bad. The Japanese were well covered in every part of the city, and the street fighting was horrible. The Japanese were dug in well, and they had all kinds of firepower; there were mines all over the place, and small weapons fire came from everywhere. After Manila Bay, we received orders to chase the Japanese north to Aparri. We had to cut out our own roads through the jungle so we could move all our vehicles. At first, everything was going well, but then all hell opened up on us. We were ambushed. Mortar and rifle fire came from all around us. We all left our vehicles for cover, and I remember Ed telling me that we must stay together. We ran off the road and tried to take cover in the tall grass, but we suddenly realized that was where the rifle fire was coming from. All of a sudden, everything was still—it was an eerie quiet. In the distance, we noticed a cover that looked like a door made of grass; it was a Japanese pillbox. We could barely see a head that looked out. It was a sniper. Ed said to me, 'Angelo, you've got to get him.' I had a .30 caliber carbine, and I was an expert on the range at base training, so it was up to me. We were all scared stiff. I took aim, and when he stuck his head out again, I fired. I hit him square in the head.

"We waited a long while before we decided to go ahead and check to see if I had killed him. When I finally got to the pillbox, I kicked it up and fired a few more shots. The sniper was dead with a bullet hole in the head. I remember he was wearing a new uniform, and when I searched him I found pictures of his family—a wife, two girls, and a son. About that time, Ed came. He took a long look at the photos and we looked at each other, not saying a word for several minutes. We each had our own thoughts, but I'm sure they were the same, and they never left us."

P.O.W. "It was starting to get dark when we headed down toward the road to catch up to our company. But there was noise coming from the road, a Japanese patrol. We hid in the high grass, and Ed said he had a plan. 'Don't fire at them until they're all past us,' he said. 'I'll fire first.' We waited until they got past us. Bang. Ed started to fire, and we all fired. We caught them by surprise, and they scattered out of sight into the high grass. But more Japanese heard the firing and out of nowhere came down on us in waves. I looked at Ed, and he said we should all split up, and we all headed in different directions. Ed went to the right and I moved to the left. I thought I was moving away from the Japanese, but I went right into their trap. Two Japanese hit me in my back with their rifles, and when I staggered to my feet, I was a P.O.W.

"They hit me with their rifle butts and kicked me. They took my weapon away and marched me to their base camp. When they found the dead sniper, they beat me again with their rifles. When we got to their camp, they put me into a bamboo hut built like a prison. I had to take off all my clothes, and I was left nude for two days without food or water. One morning, a Japanese officer started to ask me questions in what English he knew. My reply was only my rank and serial number. They called me a murderer and kicked me around whenever they felt like it. This went on for two months. I lost twenty-five pounds, but I tried to keep my mind active with prayer. I also paid attention each day to the movements of the guards. One morning, I realized there were no guards around. Nowhere. That's when I escaped. I was lucky to find the road and then a convoy that was headed to Aparri. I got miraculously back to our outfit and caught up to Ed again. When I got back with my company, I cried and cried every night, thinking of those Japanese kids whose father I shot. But Ed was always there for me. He kept me sane; if he were not around, I would have flipped."

Stateside. "When we eventually got to Wakayama, Japan, the war was nearly over. We were given orders to go home, and when we arrived in the states, Ed and I made plans to get together after we got organized. But we never did. Ed was a great guy, a real leader, and he was respected by all of us. We made a great team. Ed was such a kind person, always helping someone, and I'll never forget him. His values, they were pretty solid, very solid in fact. I'll always believe that prayer kept Ed and me from going completely off our rockers. Prayer saw us home safely; God was with us. The day we arrived back home was the last time I saw Ed. For years, I wrote Ed letters to try to get together, but he never answered them."

Over the years, the trauma of war has resulted in a combination of psychological symptoms that has been given different names over time. In the Civil War, it was known as "soldier's heart," and during World Wars I and II, it was called "shell shock," "battle fatigue," and "hidden enemy." After the Vietnam War, it became known as "post-tramatic stress disorder," PTSD.

Classified as an anxiety disorder, PTSD refers to trauma outside the normal human experience. "PTSD is when you're exposed to some life-threatening situation and your initial response is terror, overwhelming emotions, and helplessness," according to Ed Klama, Vietnam War veteran and PTSD program coordinator at Edward J. Hines Jr. Veterans Administration Hospital near Chicago. "That's the first part of PTSD, exposure to a trauma and your subjective reaction. After that, your overwhelming emotional response gets played out through intrusive thoughts, nightmares, insomnia, depression, a variety of symptoms. People make an adjustment in the midst of trauma or combat in that they turn down their emotions so a lot of emotional reaction is suppressed. Later on, when they're in a safer environment and they have time to reflect on what they've experienced, that's when PTSD, the post-traumatic stress disorder, shows itself."

Eddie Waitkus, soldier-athlete, survived many life-threatening traumatic experiences. As an infantryman, he lost his youth in war. And as a star baseball player, when he acknowledged a strange plea from a stranger—"I realize that this is a little out of the ordinary, but as I said, it's rather important. Please come soon. I won't take up much of your time"—his future was shattered. When baseball was no longer with him, he slipped emotionally, and slowly over the years, his life was defined by disorders and features associated with PTSD: Waitkus suffered from major depression, anxiety, insomnia, avoidance, feelings of detachment or estrangement from others, marital conflict, divorce, loss of job, and self-medicating alcohol abuse.

Waitkus once told his son, "My trust level became a whole lot less after I was shot than before. . . . You take what life gives you. Things happen for a purpose." This fatalistic view of life, according to Dr. Jerry Zadecki, the chief of the PTSD clinic at Hines V.A. Hospital, is prevalent in many people who suffer from PTSD: "People who have PTSD develop some kind of belief system that is kind of sarcastic, cynical, or pessimistic because they have lost their positive, optimistic view of life. The trauma has shaken the basic positive assumption about life, about the goodness of other people, and also about self-worth. We basically function as normal people on the basis of positive, maybe naive, assumptions that life is meaningful. But these people who were exposed to what we call trauma lost this positive, naive set of beliefs. They lost the basic, positive assumption about themselves, about others, and about the positive meaning of life."

After Waitkus and his wife separated, Carol said Waitkus could not face his past or present responsibilities. "He refused to get help," Carol said. "He was in denial, about his depression and about his drinking. Not playing for those three years he was in the war, and then coming back only to be shot in a hotel room, it had a tremendous impact on him."

"Stress is cumulative," said Klama. "You're involved in a war, and it takes a certain amount of your reserve to deal with that. Then you're physically attacked and shot by someone, and it takes a little bit more of your reserve to deal with that. Then you lose your job, you're out of baseball, and you lose your marriage, and it takes more out of you. So increasingly you become less capable of dealing with stress."

Living away from his family was very difficult for Waitkus. He saw Ronni and Ted only occasionally, at holidays and on family birthdays. He always tried to be optimistic whenever he saw his kids. On one such visit, Waitkus admitted to his son that he saw himself as Pagliacci, from the Italian opera where the leading characters see their tragic roles become real. "I'm a sad clown, happy on the outside, making people laugh," he said. "But inside I'm crying."

According to PTSD research, many people who struggle with the disorder develop a facade. This way they can avoid dealing with sensitive questions about their trauma. "They put on a cheerful, happy face," said Klama. "But behind that wall, they're vulnerable. And they try to avoid anything that would breach that wall."

When Eddie Waitkus met Carol Webel on Clearwater Beach in November 1949, he found inspiration, someone who, as he said, was always there to cheer him on. And in 1961, months after losing Carol, Eddie suffered what his doctors called a "nervous breakdown."

"Basically, after the shooting, she cured him," said Dr. Zadecki. "She gave him support, she gave him some kind of balance in his life, and he eventually lost her. Divorce isn't trauma, it is a stress. But for people like him, who went through traumatic events, there's a cumulative effect. PTSD can resurface or surface for the first time even twenty years after the traumatic incident. When all the support system disappears, people can experience PTSD symptoms in a very strong way."

Recent PTSD research and data suggested that PTSD symptoms and substance abuse not only emerge simultaneously but follow a relatively parallel course over time. Many professional baseball players in Waitkus's era drank. His good friend, Russ Meyer, according to Mary Meyer Oswalt, went to the mound several times after drinking episodes. Waitkus always drank socially, but after baseball he became a loner, trying to drink away his depression. "That's part of the avoidance, I think, not wanting to experience the feelings," explained Klama. "And with the use of substances like alcohol, that takes on a life of its own. It's progressive, so it would gradually get worse and worse, and pretty soon the alcohol would be the primary problem."

On the wall above Dr. Zadecki's desk, a small plaque reads: "All Wounds Aren't Visible." "Visible to other people," he noted. "It means there is something inside, something that you can't change, basically the memory. A Vietnam veteran brought it to my office, and it's a good reminder. Even though a person doesn't experience full-blown PTSD, the memory of the traumatic event—internally—is still very painful. The wounds aren't visible because the truth is that most people with PTSD can function socially. But they have difficulty establishing meaningful relationships, have difficulty holding onto jobs, and have difficulty in a competitive society. They are outcasts, somewhat withdrawn; they bunker themselves, and they suffer. This is completely invisible to other people."

Waitkus's psychological wounds were never visible: he drank but was not seen as a drunk; he was depressed yet functioned professionally; he was noncommunicative at home but loved and cherished his wife and children until his hidden enemy kept them forever apart.

17

The Pleasure of Your Own

They stood in small groups throughout the ballroom in Philadelphia's Warwick Hotel. They held their drinks and laughed and told stories about the good old days. It was June 1963, and the Whiz Kids reminisced about their 1950 National League championship. Eddie Sawyer, who the aging players still called "Skip," smoked a big cigar and held court at the bar; Richie Ashburn, who had become a Phillies radio broadcaster, amused a group in another area; and an animated Eddie Waitkus pounded his fists and told a gathering, "I tell you, this team won the pennant on guts and desire."

The Phillies management turned the reunion into a first-class event. Sawyer and his men were honored with a parade, and the Whiz Kids faced the current Phillies team in an exhibition contest before a night game at Connie Mack Stadium. Jim Konstanty, the Magician, stole the show during the pregame ceremonies when he arrived in a helicopter that dropped him off at home plate.

Waitkus was living in Waltham, Massachusetts, with his sister, Stella, when the Whiz Kids reunited; he was selling sporting goods at the Grover Cronin department store. As always, he wanted to present a good appearance to his old teammates, and this meant attending with his family. "It was all very exciting, and dad was very insistent we went as a family," said Ronni. "He was pretty nervous. I think his nervousness was because people there didn't know he and mom were separated."

"Eddie didn't seem sure of himself at first, a little on edge," recalled Maje McDonnell, the Whiz Kids' batting practice pitcher. "But when he saw everybody, he let it out a bit, just like the old Eddie. Not too many people saw him after that, though."

Not long after the Whiz Kids reunion, Waitkus moved out of his sister's home and returned to Cambridge, where he rented a room on the second floor of Belle Powers's modest home at 14 Fayette Street; the house was divided into many rooms to accommodate students from nearby Harvard University. It sat on a quiet, tree-lined street where neighborhood kids played ball during the day, and all the homes turned dark well before midnight.

"Eddie was such a pleasant person," Powers said. "He was always very quiet, never went out at night. He'd stay in his room at night and read his books and had his drinks. I would tell him, 'when you're through, come on down for some chowder,' and he would, and we would talk and talk. I don't think he had any close friends, except for the kids around here. I think his friends were really the kids. He'd play ball with them in the street, and then he'd go down to Cambridge Field and play more ball."

Steve Buckley, sports columnist for the *Boston Herald,* grew up on Fayette Street. "We were street kids," Buckley recalled. "We'd go down to the courtyard at Longfellow Grammar School and play spongeball. We drew a strike zone on the school's red brick and try to hit one over the wrought-iron fence to Broadway Street. Eddie would stop by and give us hitting tips. I was mesmerized by baseball as a kid, and Eddie was the first or second major leaguer I ever met."

Waitkus spent the last several years of his life in a rented room in Powers's home. For a short time, he worked as a surveyor for Middlesex County, and from time to time, he visited the Lithuanian clubs in Cambridge. But mostly, he stayed in his room on Fayette Street. He lost all contact with his baseball buddies, and although he had moved back to Cambridge, he never looked up his old friends. "We grew up together in East Cambridge, and we were real buddies," remembered Frank Sharka. "We did everything together. We double-dated on our senior prom. I remember Eddie gave me my first TV set when they threw that night for him in Philly after he was shot. He was always such a happy-go-lucky kind of guy. But after baseball, I never saw him. A few of us tried to find him, but he'd always duck you."

Only once did Waitkus call a friend to try to get back into baseball. Lennie Merullo knew Waitkus had a drinking problem, but he was also a friend; so when Waitkus called, Merullo said he would try to help. In the early 1960s, Merullo was the New England scout for the Chicago Cubs, and he arranged for Waitkus to meet Cubs superscout Ray Hayworth. "Maybe Eddie and Ray would hit it off and Eddie could get back into baseball," he said. Merullo, however, knew Waitkus's reputation as a drinker would not sit well with the conservative Cubs management. Merullo and his wife, Jean, invited Waitkus and Hayworth to their Reading, Massachusetts, home for dinner, hoping the two men would hit it off. Waitkus didn't drink that evening and, as always, was witty and charming. But after dinner, Hayworth told Merullo he didn't think Chicago's front office would go for the idea; Waitkus's chances of rejoining the Cubs organization never got beyond Merullo's dining room. Waitkus had been right when he told Carol years earlier there was no sentiment in baseball. That night at Merullo's was the last time Waitkus ever made an effort to get back into big league baseball.

For all his struggles, Waitkus was remarkably communicative with youngsters. "He used to talk with my kids about baseball all the time and even took them to see the Red Sox play," said Powers. "He loved his own children. He'd write them a lot, especially his daughter. She was so beautiful." Waitkus was an accomplished, highly intelligent man, who, as his life began to slip, could no longer communicate with his wife, the person closest to him, but he could connect with kids.

"People who have a difficulty communicating with their peers, wives, or coworkers because of their defenses and a lack of trust are much more open to children," according to Dr. Zadecki. "I have diagnosed people with PTSD who have developed very meaningful relationships with the next generation, the children. It becomes a way for them to pay back, because they feel guilty by themselves. Basically, it's a very positive part of their recovery process to be connected with anybody."

Although Waitkus lived by himself the last several years of his life, he became connected with a new generation of ballplayers in 1967. Forty-five minutes south of Boston, near a place called Loon Pond, Waitkus returned to his youth as a baseball coach and counselor at the Ted Williams Camp. The tiny town of Lakeville, a woodsy, sleepy village of spring-fed waters, offered Waitkus a baseball sanctuary where he could reconnect and redefine his unraveling life. The Ted Williams Camp proved to be a worthy retreat for Waitkus.

"I always knew Eddie Waitkus was a great ballplayer, but he was a hell of a man, too," said Ted Williams. "The kids at the camp loved him. He was magnificent with them, and we were truly lucky to have him. He was a classy-looking hitter and a classy-looking fielder. I loved that camp, being around the kids, teaching baseball. And I know Eddie did too."

In the late 1960s, the Ted Williams Camp was the Yankee Stadium of the baseball camp world. Each summer, more than two hundred boys from all fifty states and from as far away as Japan, England, Switzerland, France, and Puerto Rico made the trek to the serenity of the Massachusetts woods to improve their baseball skills, the Ted Williams way. Located a quarter of a mile from the nearest road, the camp was devoted solely to baseball. "That in itself was extraordinary," said Steve Ferroli, a longtime Williams aide. "You were in the middle of God's country, and there was nothing around but baseball. All the activity focused on baseball. The kids never went out, and when they weren't playing baseball, they were talking baseball."

Waitkus found comfort in the camp's military spit-and-polish atmosphere. As Williams said, "In order to do things right in an operation like this, you have to be firm." Waitkus was the hitting instructor, quite an honor when you think that the camp was run by perhaps the greatest hitter ever. "Eddie was just so great with the kids," Williams said.

Because all the age groups passed through the hitting cage, everyone got to know Eddie—campers, counselors, and coaches. He was very exposed at the camp; this was not an environment where he could avoid people. "He spent some really good years there," said Carol. "He had a closeness with the kids, and that helped him. It was a good spot for Eddie."

Waitkus bunked in the camp's front cabin, near the largest of the five baseball diamonds. On mornings he was designated O.D.—Officer of the Day—Waitkus walked into each cabin throughout the camp and shouted, "Time to get up. Are you ready? Who's going to get better today?" The Ted Williams Camp clearly was a safe house for Waitkus. It forced him to stay in the present; it kept him centered. It gave him the opportunity to connect and become communicative again. Baseball, the ultimate here-and-now game, re-entered his life when he needed it the most, and once again, it filled his days.

Each morning, the campers, counselors, and coaches walked from their cabins through the woods and trudged up a large hill where they ate breakfast in a dinning hall that overlooked a crystal-clear lake. On that daily trek, kids often approached Waitkus for some one-on-one advice. "In that 150-yard walk to breakfast, whether you're Ted Williams, Eddie Waitkus, or Steve

Ferroli, you're open game for the kids, and they all wanted your individual attention," said Ferroli. "It made you feel like a kid again, answering all their questions. They were like memory missiles the way they came at you, and Eddie was great at talking with the kids." One of those kids was Mark Shapiro. "He was an unbelievably unassuming guy," Shapiro recalled. "At first, I had no idea he was a past pro ballplayer. He never talked about his life, but he became an uncle to all of us."

Baseball players have a technical love for the game, especially when it comes to their particular position. "We used to love to have him demonstrate plays at first base," Shapiro said. "His footwork was a lost art. He was so effortless, and he was so unique at communicating. He must have loved the horses because he had nicknames for everyone. I played shortstop; he called me 'Whirlaway.' And he called the pitcher 'Citation.' Having him go through the moves at first base, it was wonderful."

Looking much older than his fifty years, Waitkus still glided with familiarity and ease on the camp's stone dust infield. He fielded ground balls and caught an assortment of less-than-accurate throws from the teenage players. Long ago, a skinny Eddie Waitkus watched in awe as Jack Burns performed the same magic at Cambridge Field. Waitkus's routine never wavered. He scooped up each grounder, gracefully tagged the bag, and fired a missile that stung the hand of the kid who caught the ball at home plate. "Some people think the first baseman ought to pay his way into the ball game because all he has to do is catch a thrown ball," he told the youngsters as he moved to the bag. "Sometimes catching that ball is pretty much of a task. Take Whirlaway over there at shortstop. He throws a sinking curveball and a fastball that takes off. You have to adjust. And what about that grounder in the hole? It's the hardest job for a first baseman, to move toward second, grab the skidding ball, square around and throw to the pitcher covering first. If Citation gets off the mound quickly, the job is easy. But it takes a lot of practice."

It began as a simple baseball drill, a game of pepper one hot afternoon on the camp's high school diamond, but it drew special attention because of the participants—Ted Williams hitting and Eddie Waitkus fielding. The routine started quietly. Waitkus threw strikes, and Williams stroked accommodating one-hoppers, ten, maybe fifteen softies that were easily handled. It was an exercise in baseball technique, nothing more. But as word of the game spread, a large group of kids and coaches gathered around, and the pepper picked up speed. Waitkus's throws suddenly had more zip to them, and Williams's one-hoppers turned to line drives. Waitkus snared everything Williams hit, including the smashes right at his feet. Twenty, twenty-five swings now, and Waitkus caught each ball cleanly. And Williams's hits were laser-true. The campers and counselors had formed a quiet, tense semicircle around the former major leaguers. Ted Williams, they knew, hated to lose, at anything. But what about Waitkus, this quiet, ex-pro nobody really knew well. How long would he stay there, calmly dismissing the rockets off the bat of Ted Williams? There, in the wilds of Massachusetts, the best hitter of his generation dueled one of the game's finest-fielding first baseman. But what honor was at stake? With one shot, Williams finally crossed the line. His last swing shot the ball toward Waitkus's head. Waitkus twisted his body and threw his glove hand in front of his face to protect himself. "To hell with this," he muttered under his breath. He flipped his glove toward Williams and walked off the diamond. Only when the glove hit the infield dirt did the ball roll out of the pocket.

When the summer sun disappeared beyond Loon Pond and the baseball stopped, only the distant jabber of the crickets could be heard across the diamonds. The nights were a tough adjustment for many of the campers. Waitkus knew about lonely nights. "I didn't like being away from home," Shapiro remembered. "During the day it was fun because of baseball and all the activity, but at night, it was hard. Having Eddie there really helped. He was like a surrogate father to us. We could always go to him if we had any problems. He was older than most of the coaches at the camp, and everyone went to him for advice."

Waitkus played baseball in an era when players talked baseball everywhere—on train rides, in hotel lobbies, in the clubhouse; they read the *Sporting News,* not *Business Week.* The Ted Williams Camp was a throwback to Waitkus's playing days. "When night arrived, the real baseball players came out," Ferroli said. "Most cabins had a ball game on TV, and in others, the kids talked baseball until they fell asleep. Eddie loved that. He'd be right in there with them, demonstrating a batting stance or how to cover the bag." Many of the campers didn't know Waitkus was a one-time big league star. "He was so private, but caring," Shapiro said. "He always told us, 'Do your talking on the field.'"

In June 1969, Waitkus received his final major league honor. Fans in Philadelphia selected Waitkus as the greatest first baseman in Phillies' history. The voting was held in celebration of the first one hundred years of baseball. Waitkus left the camp and returned to Philadelphia where he was given a commemorative plaque in a ceremony before a Phillies night game. Baseball writer Sandy Grady reported:

"Eddie Waitkus swirled the beer in the paper cup and stared through the lights at the field where so much of it happened, 19 years ago. Ramrod straight and somber at 49, Waitkus was damned if he had come back to be embarrassed or to laugh at this thing. Waitkus does not laugh easily."

Waitkus beat out home run slugger Rich Allen, a popular, albeit controversial, member of the 1969 Phillies. "It was a popularity contest," Waitkus said. "In essence, it proved one thing—the love affair between the people of Philadelphia and the Whiz Kids does not die quickly." The kids at the Ted Williams Camp were proud when their coach then said: "It was a vote for first baseman, remember, and I'm a better one than Allen. Not just fifteen years ago. Right now. Hit Allen and me fifty ground balls and I'll handle them better. And I'll bet you."

Waitkus was given a hero's welcome when he returned to Lakeville. The camp chef baked a specially decorated cake, and all the campers and staff surprised Waitkus with a party in the dining hall. "Everyone was hooting and hollering when he came into the room," said former coach Fred Brown. "The kids presented Eddie with a book about the first one hundred years of baseball and a set of bronze bookends, and then they gave him a standing ovation. Eddie told everyone, 'this is where my real friends are.'"

The last several years of Waitkus's life were defined by the Ted Williams Camp. Ted Waitkus stayed with his dad at the camp for a week each August. "I spent five days with him that last summer," Ted Waitkus said. "Historically, he liked to drink beer, but that summer he didn't. He was noticeably older-looking. He had a bad hip and walked with a cane, and his hairline was receding. Still, he was a great hitting instructor, even with the cane. He was great at articulating how to hit a baseball. We'd play catch most of the time. He'd get me Louisville Sluggers with my name on them—'Eddie Waitkus Jr.' He'd tell me stories about Mickey Mantle, Ralph Houk, Ted Williams. We'd watch games together, and he'd point out the little things, especially the way the players moved. The common thread between us was baseball. He was my hero."

Well past midnight, after the baseball talk stopped and the campers were asleep, Waitkus's thoughts drifted. He was plagued by sleepless nights; when sleep did come it was restless at best. During the days, he told his children, there's baseball to pass the time, but late at night, when the memories take hold, the hours drag by. On many nights, a soft, yellow glow from his cabin was visible until dawn as a father struggled with his past. On one particular night, his daughter, Ronni, was on his mind:

Glamorous graduate, fidgety freshman,

It's hard to realize that the lovely lady in the cap and gown, and the boy with the mischievous smile in the photographs once crawled across the floor to get a better look at TV. Suddenly they are young adults.

Each morning (5:30) starts with bewilderment as each glance at your picture makes me wonder where the years have gone. The kids in baseball camp are fun, but small compensation for the pleasure of your own.

Well, brat, you've gone through another door in the house of life. It's a hard time of life, making all the adjustments you are called upon to make now. In years to come, all the things that are so important now may become trivial to you, but only time will prove that to you. Through the years I've found that I'd rather have the happiness of victories, checkered with the heartaches of defeats, than to have lived in a twilight zone of grays, and enjoyed neither. And I guess my life has been filled with both. Migawd, am I on the soap-box!

Despite the lapse of time I can find so little to write about from this end. My hip came along well, and I am again taking batting practice with the boys. I couldn't get out much last winter, with the horrible weather and a cane, and it was pretty lonely and miserable.

Your mother's pictures are self-explanatory. She's looking extremely well.

I'm physically and mentally tired. How'd you like this for a schedule? I give 21 half-hour lectures a week, manage a team in 10 games a week, and am hitting instructor for the whole camp. The one good thing about it is that you stumble into bed ready for sleep, without your mind reliving the past.

I hope when you get here you'll have time for an occasional dinner with your old man who loves you so much, even though his correspondence doesn't always show it. I'll try to be handy to help in any way I can but you won't find me interfering or stifling the great years I hope you'll be having.

All my love,
Your square, square father

P.S. The enclosed poem ["If"] I thought you'd like.

18

Lost Hero

The Ted Williams Camp allowed Waitkus to pass the baseball part of his life on to a new generation. Although he was away from those closest to him, his wife and children, he found a resurgence at the camp late in his life. "But his days were blending into each other," his daughter, Ronni, recalled. "He had a great loss of not regularly seeing my brother and me. He would write me from the camp, asking me to write. I know he was depressed, and I think he would always write his letters at night. He was getting a real sense that his life was shortening."

In the summer of 1972, life was catching up to Waitkus. The previous year, he had fractured his hip when he fell from the second story while installing storm windows at Belle Powers's home in Cambridge. Waitkus lost his balance, tumbled from a second-story ledge, and landed on his feet, severely jarring his hip. The injury healed slowly, and when he arrived at camp, he walked with a painful limp. His health deteriorated rapidly during that summer. The New England sun painted his face a healthy-looking tan, but it was nothing more than a facade. Waitkus was weary and had little energy, and his eyes were sunken; nearing his fifty-third year, he carried the look of an old man. Waitkus's persistent cough worsened and he had difficulty breathing at times. Although he had quit drinking, he still smoked daily. "His Benson and Hedges Menthol 100s never left his side," his son, Ted, remembered. "Dad was recuperating from a broken hip during his last year at the camp, and he walked with a pronounced limp. But there he was, cane and all, teaching kids how to hit."

Waitkus felt so poorly, he left Lakeville in late August—one week before camp broke—and drove back to Cambridge, unaware of the indolent cancer that was about to take his life. Within days of returning home, he entered the Veterans Administration hospital in Jamaica Plain. Like his mother, he suffered from pneumonia, and like his mother, he never left the hospital. "I saw him at the hospital," Ronni said. "He looked tired, but he actually had some color. You could tell he'd been out in the sun. He was always philosophical, especially about us. He had this thing about women. The very last thing he said to me was, 'Ronni, you can't make class. When you walk into a room you either have it or you don't. If you do, that can mean everything, especially for a girl.' I left him that night thinking it was a morbid conversation. But I was nineteen, and I didn't pay much attention to it."

Two days later, Ronni's aunt Stella called her at college to say her father was gone. In the first hour of September 16, 1972, twelve days after his fifty-third birthday, Waitkus died from esophageal cancer. His death was a shock to his family and his friends at the camp; no one knew he had cancer. An autopsy revealed cancer of the esophagus and lungs, according to Waitkus's family. In a letter to the campers and counselors, Bernie Cassidy, the executive director of the Ted Williams Camp, wrote:

> On Wednesday, September 13, I spent an hour with Eddie Waitkus at the Veterans Administration Hospital in Jamaica Plain, Boston, Mass. Ed had just had a biopsy done on Tuesday, but in spite of this, his spirits were great. He proudly showed me the insurmountable stacks of Get Well Wishes from all of you. In Ed's own words, he said, 'When I am feeling better, I intend to answer each one of these with my own personal Thank You. I really appreciate this.' I left Ed that day feeling that with the continuance of mail and his great spirit and desire he was going to make it. Ed's family was with him on Thursday evening and left him after visiting hours with no indication that the end was in sight for Ed. He took a turn for the worse and at 1:00 A.M. Friday [Saturday], Ed struck out.

Waitkus's wake was held at the modest Waitkus Funeral Home, about a block away from Cambridge Field. His family was not associated with the funeral home, but the funeral home certainly was a part of his past. As a boy, Waitkus more than once answered the telephone in the middle of the night at his home on Portland Street and said, "No, we can't come over and pick up the body. This isn't the Waitkus mortuary." Waitkus loved telling this story.

Parlor A was filled with Eddie's closest friends from the Ted Williams Camp, including Bernie Cassidy, Fred and Marge Brown, and Ted Ciesla. Campers from all over the Boston area and from as far away as Rhode Island and New Hampshire attended the crowded wake with their families. Eddie's family was there, as well as Belle Powers and his boyhood friends from East Cambridge. So was Steve Buckley and his Fayette Street pals. "We felt we owed it to him," Buckley said. "After all, he taught us how to hit." Waitkus belonged to the V.F.W. Ferricane Post 3275 in East Cambridge; three post officers placed a flag on his coffin, along with a red rose and a white carnation. Representation from major league baseball, however, was conspicuously absent. After eleven years in the big leagues, only two former players paid their respects—the Phillies' Ed Pellagrini and the Cubs' Lennie Merullo. "There were no letters of condolences to our family from the Phillies or the Cubs or from major leaguer baseball," said Ted Waitkus. "Nothing."

Following a memorial service at Immaculate Conception Lithuanian Catholic Church, the long funeral procession wound its way its way past leafy Harvard University on its way to Cambridge Cemetery. "Well, Eddie finally made Harvard," someone remarked. As a late summer thunderstorm soaked the earth, Eddie Waitkus was buried in the middle of a long row of markers in the cemetery's World War II section. Members of a military unit performed a rifle volley followed by taps, and the V.F.W. officers carefully folded the American flag from the coffin into a tricorner and presented it to Waitkus's son. The flat, gray marker at Tier 22-Grave 31 reads:

Edward Waitkus
Massachusetts
CPL U.S. Army
World War II
September 4, 1919–September 16, 1972

On a Tuesday night in August 1952, the Phillies edged the Reds 4–3 at Shibe Park. It was just one of 1,140 major league games he played in, but it symbolized the style that was Eddie Waitkus. He went four-for-four, drove home the tying run, scored the winning run, and was perfect at first base. His performance prompted a Cincinnati writer to report, "He's the best in the league." Frank Yeutter was also impressed, and under the headline "Easy-Does-It Eddie Waitkus Is Just an All-Around Good Guy at First Base," wrote: "Maybe Gil Hodges and Ted Kluszewski can hit for greater distance; old timers will say Joe Kuhel was a fancier Dan around the bag; Charlie Grimm had the greatest pair of hands; Whitey Lockman can run faster—but mix a jigger of each into one concoction and it's Eddie Waitkus." In eleven major league seasons, Waitkus batted .285 and his fielding average was a sparkling .993. From his sandlot days at Cambridge Field to the big leagues, Waitkus was an all star at every level he ever played.

It was his quiet, classy persona, however, that people remember about him. "He was never loud, but he had this way of getting his message across," said Russ Meyer. As a Cubs' rookie in 1946, Waitkus was sent sprawling at the plate when Dodgers' pitcher Kirby Higbe, on orders from manager Leo Durocher, fired a pitch high and inside. "Wake this busher up," Durocher barked from the dugout. On the next pitch, Waitkus hit a line drive that rolled all the way to the Wrigley Field ivy in center for a triple. The next inning, as the Cubs took warm-ups, Durocher made his way to the first-base coaching box. Stan Hack let loose with a throw from third but Waitkus was deliberately tardy in reacting; the ball sailed past Durocher's head and into the Brooklyn dugout. "Gosh, I'm sorry, Mr. Durocher, that one got away from me," Waitkus said.

Richie Ashburn always thought Waitkus was a cut above most major leaguers. "He wasn't the regular, normal ballplayer," Ashburn once said of his teammate. "He wasn't a rough guy; he wasn't a nasty guy. He didn't go in with his spikes high, and he didn't fight. He was almost an aberration. He read Latin, loved poetry and classical music, and was an expert in ball-room dancing. Sometimes, looking back at his other talents and interests, I used to think it was a shame he had to play baseball."

As a young, confident ballplayer, Waitkus, as his sister, Stella, said, was "happy-go-lucky and full of life." He took whatever life presented, surviving war and the nearly fatal obsession of a troubled girl. But without baseball and away from his family, Waitkus was lost. "It was a joy to watch Eddie play ball," Carol said. "His grace, desire, the low-keyed way about him. Eddie Waitkus was the cool professional in baseball, in the war. But he was more content not having to face all the turmoil of responsibility at the end of his life. It's sad his life wasn't different; he was probably sick for years."

The twists and turns of Waitkus's life had a lasting influence on his son. As a small boy, when his father bathed him, Ted Waitkus often placed his small fingers into two deep folds, once scars, in his dad's back, the only physical reminder of Steinhagen's obsession. In those days, Waitkus still had hope for the future, for himself, and for his family, but fate had another agenda. Through the years, the gold, diamond-studded 1945 Cubs National League championship ring became a metaphor for Waitkus's life. Once a symbol of triumph, the ring eventually found its way to a Boston pawnshop. When Waitkus's family cleared out his room on Fayette Street following his death, they found no ring. Instead, among the World War II and poetry books, biographies and science fiction novels, they discovered a pawnshop claim ticket. The ring was retrieved for Ted but was stolen from his home a few years later and lost forever.

"My dad's shooting became a tragedy after the fact: baseball camps in the summer, unemployment in the winter," Ted Waitkus said. "Ruth Ann Steinhagen was the turning point in my father's life. He once told me he thought he knew a girl named Burns from Cambridge, but who cares if he knew a girl by that name or not. Women always liked my dad, and my dad always liked women. The shooting, in one respect, calmed him down, and my mother probably would have never met him if he didn't get shot. I find it fateful that he had to go through the process. He told me mother was 'the only love in my life.' It may have been lip service, but I believe him. I would give anything for one more game of catch with my dad, just one more."

The Natural's Roy Hobbs sets out to break as many baseball records as he can: "I wanted everything . . . if you leave all those records that nobody else can beat—they'll always remember you. You sorta never die." Unlike Hobbs, Waitkus never sought the hero's role."It's amazing how one part of his life was so extraordinary, and the other part was not," Carol said. Hobbs and Waitkus experienced a haunting sense of emptiness, while people looked upon them with admiration. "My goddamn life didn't turn out like I wanted it to," Hobbs confides. As for Waitkus, his daughter, Ronni, said, "Dad was a philosophical man, always dreaming—about what he was going to do some day that he never did. Here's this poor man who a lot of people around him really didn't know. What did he want out of life? He once told me he didn't get out of life what he wanted. But what was it?"

Eddie Waitkus, baseball's original natural, survived what life threw at him—war in foreign lands and the irony of being shot in a Chicago hotel room—but he was never able to outlive his past. A lost hero to his family and friends, he will always belong to those who love baseball for its imperfect heroes, individuals who lure us into history and passionately capture us forever.

He'd like to play baseball without end,
For baseball is a real good friend.

—Written of Edward Stephen Waitkus, class of 1937,
Cambridge High and Latin School yearbook

Currently a freelance journalist and writer, John Theodore began his journalism career in 1970. He has served as a Chicago reporter, writer, editor, and television and radio producer for United Press International, WGN, and WGN-TV. A graduate of the University of Illinois at Urbana-Champaign in 1969, he is married, has three children, and lives in a suburb of Chicago.